AI
ARTIFICIAL INTELLIGENCE BASICS FOR SCHOOL STUDENTS (CLASS IX)

I0016234

N notion press
.com

INDIA · SINGAPORE · MALAYSIA

Notion Press

Old No. 38, New No. 6
McNichols Road, Chetpet
Chennai - 600 031

First Published by Notion Press 2020
Copyright © Dr. Dheeraj Mehrotra 2020
All Rights Reserved.

ISBN 978-1-64869-959-7

AI
ARTIFICIAL INTELLIGENCE
BASICS FOR
SCHOOL STUDENTS
(CLASS IX)

As per the **LATEST**
CBSE CURRICULUM (Code No. 417)

DR. DHEERAJ MEHROTRA

INDIA · SINGAPORE · MALAYSIA

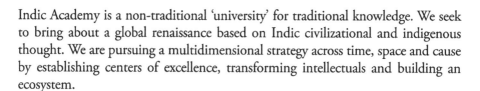

IN)ICACADEMY

INDIC PLEDGE

- *I celebrate our civilisational identity, continuity & legacy in thought, word and deed.*

- *I believe our indigenous thought has solutions for the global challenges of health, happiness, peace, and sustainability.*

- *I shall seek to preserve, protect and promote this heritage in doing so,*
  - *discover, nurture and harness my potential,*
  - *connect, cooperate and collaborate with fellow seekers,*
  - *be inclusive and respectful of diverse opinions.*

ABOUT INDIC ACADEMY

Indic Academy is a non-traditional 'university' for traditional knowledge. We seek to bring about a global renaissance based on Indic civilizational and indigenous thought. We are pursuing a multidimensional strategy across time, space and cause by establishing centers of excellence, transforming intellectuals and building an ecosystem.

Indic Academy is pleased to support this book.

Contents

Preface

Artificial Intelligence, the much talked about tech jargon has revamped our lives with **'wow'** scenario of computing and learning. The revolutionary introduction by the CBSE – Central Board of Secondary Education has paved a smart culture of learning among the schools PAN India and other countries where CBSE has its presence.

The book featuring "ARTIFICIAL INTELLIGENCE" for class IX targets learning of concepts as prescribed by the CBSE. The objective of the module is to develop a readiness for understanding and appreciating Artificial Intelligence and its application in our lives. The units dwelled include Excite, Relate, Purpose, Possibilities and AI Ethics which are set to empower the kids to identify and appreciate AI and describe its applications in daily life and to apply and reflect on the Human-Machine Interactions.

I am sure the students and the teachers would like to take it as a skill development exercise incorporating the AI Readiness through Technical and Life Skills as set objectives for introducing the course at the school level.

Happy Learning!

(Dheeraj Mehrotra)
dheerajmehrotra@icloud.com

CBSE – Department of Skill Education

ARTIFICIAL INTELLIGENCE (Code 417)

Curriculum for Class IX
(Inspire and Acquire Module)

Objective

The objective of this module/curriculum – which combines both Inspire and Acquire modules is to develop a readiness for understanding and appreciating Artificial Intelligence and its applications in our lives. This module/curriculum focuses on:

1. Helping learners understand the world of Artificial Intelligence and its applications through games, activities and multi-sensorial learning to become AI-Ready.

2. Introducing the learners to three domains of AI in an age appropriate manner.

3. Allowing the learners to construct meaning of AI through interactive participation and engaging hands-on activities.

4. Introducing the learners to AI Project Cycle.

5. Introducing the learners to programming skills – Basic Python Coding Language.

Learning Outcomes

Learners will be able to:

1. Identify and appreciate Artificial Intelligence and describe its applications in daily life.

2. Relate, apply and reflect on the Human-Machine Interactions to identify and interact with the three domains of AI: Data,

Computer Vision and Natural Language Processing and Undergo assessment for analyzing their progress towards acquired AI-Readiness skills.

3. Imagine, examine and reflect on the skills required for futuristic job opportunities.

4. Unleash their imagination towards smart homes and build an interactive story around it.

5. Understand the impact of Artificial Intelligence on Sustainable Development Goals to develop responsible citizenship.

6. Research and develop awareness of skills required for jobs of the future.

7. Gain awareness about AI bias and AI access and describe the potential ethical considerations of AI.

8. Develop effective communication and collaborative work skills.

9. Get familiar and motivated towards Artificial Intelligence and Identify the AI Project Cycle framework.

10. Learn problem scoping and ways to set goals for an AI project and understand the iterative nature of problem scoping in the AI project cycle.

11. Brainstorm on the ethical issues involved around the problem selected.

12. Foresee the kind of data required and the kind of analysis to be done, identify data requirements and find reliable sources to obtain relevant data.

13. Use various types of graphs to visualize acquired data.

14. Understand, create and implement the concept of Decision Trees.

15. Understand and visualize computer's ability to identify alphabets and handwritings.

16. Understand and appreciate the concept of Neural Network through gamification and learn basic programming skills through gamified platforms.

17. Acquire introductory Python programming skills in a very user-friendly format.

## CHAPTER 1

Introduction to AI & Gaming

What is AI?

AI is the intelligence of machines and robots and the branch of computer science that aims to create it. Artificial Intelligence is a technology and a branch of computer science that deals with the study and development of intelligent machines and software. It is the science of making a machine to think and act like an intelligent human being.

Objective of AI

The theory and development of computer systems able to perform tasks normally requiring human intelligence, such as visual perception, speech recognition, decision making and translation between language.

Features include:

a. The ability to solve problems.

b. The ability to act rationally.

c. The ability to act like humans.

History of AI

Artificial intelligence is a buzzword today, although this term is not new. In 1956, a group of avant-garde experts from different backgrounds decided to organize a summer research project on AI.

Four bright minds led the project; John McCarthy (Dartmouth College), Marvin Minsky (Harvard University), Nathaniel Rochester (IBM), and Claude Shannon (Bell Telephone Laboratories).

The primary purpose of the research project was to tackle "every aspect of learning or any other feature of intelligence that can in principle be so precisely described, that a machine can be made to simulate it."

Types of Artificial Intelligence

Artificial intelligence can be divided into three subfields:

- Artificial intelligence
- Machine learning
- Deep learning

Artificial Intelligence

Most of our smartphone, daily device or even the internet uses Artificial intelligence. Very often, AI and machine learning are used interchangeably by big companies that want to announce their latest innovation. However, Machine learning and AI are different in some ways.

Machine Learning

Machine Learning is the art of Study of Algorithms that learn from examples and experiences.

Machine learning is based on the idea that there exist some patterns in the data that were identified and used for future predictions.

The difference from hardcoding rules is that the machine learns on its own to find such rules.

Deep Learning

Deep learning is a sub-field of machine learning. Deep learning does not mean the machine learns more in-depth knowledge; it means the machine uses different layers to learn from the data. The depth of the model is represented by the number of layers in the model. For instance, Google LeNet model for image recognition counts 22 layers. In deep learning, the learning phase is done through a neural network.

Some of the most important applications of AI include the Natural Language Understanding, Expert Systems, Planning and Robotics, Machine Learning and Playing Games.

Types of Machine Learning

Machine learning is sub-categorized to three types:

- **Supervised Learning** – It is related to the concept of Work on Me! – Under this the human is teaching the learning and hence called supervised learning.

- **Unsupervised Learning** – I am happy myself in learning. The machine learns on its own.

- **Reinforcement Learning** – My Way of doing things, My rules! Here the computer uses the Hit & Trial method to do the learning.

Domains of AI

The AI learning has three domains:

a. **Data** – The facts, figures and images make a meaningful data.

b. **Computer Vision** – This directs the ability of a machine to extract information from an image that is necessary to solve a task. This works better on Image Acquisition, Image processing, Image Analysis and Image understanding.

c. **Natural Language Processing** – This is to design and build software that will analyse, understand and generate languages that human use naturally.

Artificial Intelligence/Natural Intelligence

This Is with reference to the differenciation with reference to AI. The AI is:

a. Non Creative

b. Precise

c. Consistency

d. Multitasking

Whereas the Natural Intelligence is:

a. Creative

b. May contain errors

c. Non Consistent

d. Not easy to handle.

Recommended Activity: The AI Game

Learners are to participate in three games based on different AI Domains:

The objective and the learning outcome is to relate, apply and reflect on the Human-Machine Interactions.

And to identify and interact with the three domains of AI:

Data, Computer Vision and Natural Language Processing.

The three domains of learning:

a. Data

b. Natural Language Processing

c. Computer Vision

In order to understand the above domains better we have the following three games to be conducted online as follows:

a. Rock – Paper – Scissors – This game is based on data.

b. Identify the Mystery Animal – This game is based on Natural Language Processing (NLP)

c. Emoji Scavenger Hunt – This game is based on Computer Vision

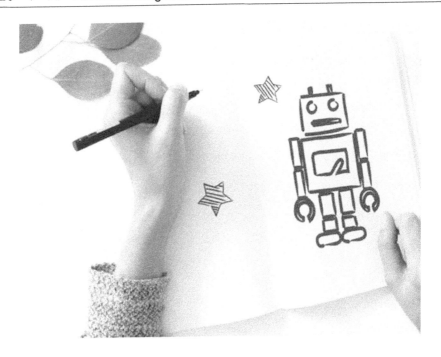

Let us play the same to understand AI better:

a. Rock – Paper – Scissors

Visit: http://bit.ly/iai4yrps

We get the screen as follows:

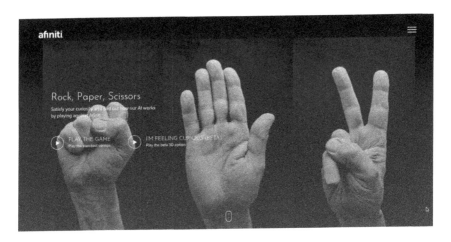

We click here:

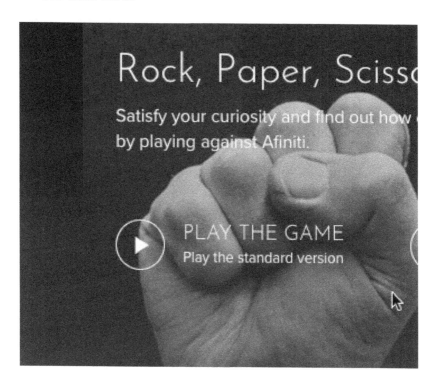

To play the game:

A screen appears as follows:

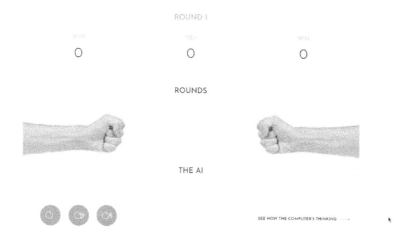

So after 11 rounds we have the result as follows:

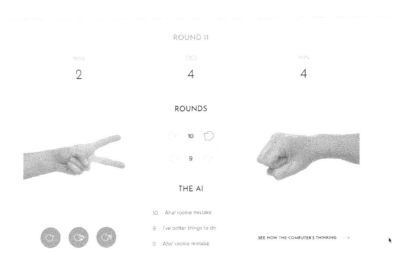

We observe here that the Rock-Paper-Scissors game explains the basic principles of an adaptive AI Technology. The Computer here learns to identify patterns of a person's behavior by analyzing his decision making and improves on its score accordingly.

b. Identify the Mystery Animal

Visit:

http://bit.ly/iai4yma   OR   https://experiments.withgoogle.com/mystery-animal

The Mystery Animal as the name says is a new spin of 20 questions game. Here the computer pretends to be an animal and the user has to guess what it is using his or her voice.

Questions like yes-or no can be asked like "Do you have feathers?," "Can you fly?," "Can you Swim?" One can play it on a Google Home by saying "Hay Google, talk to Mystery Animal" or try here on the website using the above link.

It has the following screen:

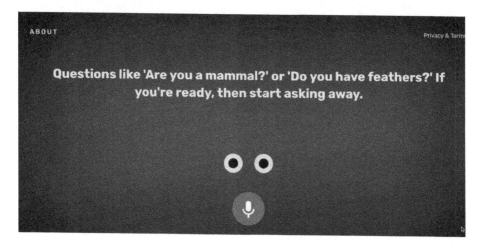

We ask the questions and computer answers the mystery animal within 20 turns. It again gives the option to ask if the identification is not done after giving the right answer.

The concept explains about the voice recognition feature of AI in learning.

c. Emoji Scavenger Hunt Game

This game explains the use of Computer Vision using the AI concept in our lives.

We go to the following website:

https://emojiscavengerhunt.withgoogle.com

And we get the following screen:

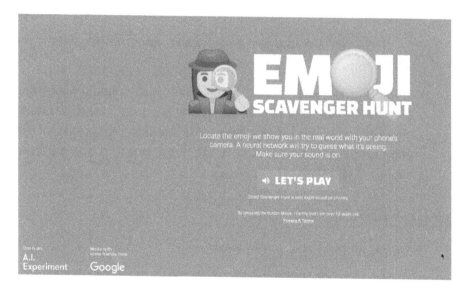

This is used to scan the images and guest what it is seeing using the Neural Network based image recognition feature of AI.

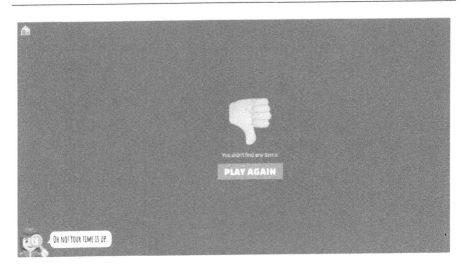

We can start this AI Experiment by clicking on "Let's Play."

It checks the images and speaks accordingly within the given time.

It is a browser based game built with machine learning that uses your phone's or computer's camera and a neural network to try and guess what it is seeing. This is one of the very simple examples of how machine learning can be used for fun in our lives.

EXERCISE

1. Write about the following in brief:

   a. Artificial Intelligence

   b. History of AI

   c. John Mc Carthy

   d. Types of AI

   e. Types of Machine Learning

2. Explain the Domains of AI.

3. What do you mean by Supervised Learning?

4. What do you mean by Unsupervised Learning?

5. Explain the term Reinforcement Learning?

6. Give the use of the following:

   a. Deep Learning

   b. Machine Learning

7. How does Machine Learning differ from Deep Learning.

8. Name the various subfields of AI.

9. Name the FOUR people responsible for the development of AI.

10. Fill In the blanks:

   a. _____ is a technology and a branch of computer science that deals with the study and development of intelligent machines and software.

   b. AI Stands for _____

   c. Artificial intelligence can be divided into _____ subfields.

   d. _____ is the art of Study of Algorithms that learn from examples and experiences.

   e. Deep learning is a sub-field of _____.

   f. _____ Learning is related to the concept of Work on Me!

   g. Reinforcement Learning relates to _____ of doing things.

   h. The three domains of AI are _____, _____ and _____.

11. Name the three domains of learning of AI.

   • Give the use of the following games with respect to AI:

   a. Rock-Paper – Scissors

   b. Identify the Mystery Animal

   c. Emoji Scavenger Hunt

12. Explain the application of AI in using the following games:

    a. Emoji Scavenger Hunt

    b. Identify the Mystery Animal.

    c. Rock – Paper – Scissor

13. Fill in the blanks:

    a. The three domains of learning via AI are: _____, _____ and _____.

    b. Emoji Scavenger Hunt game is based on _____.

    c. Rock – Paper Scissors game is based on _____.

    d. _____ is based on Natural Language Processing (NLP).

    e. _____ game explains the basic principle of an Adaptive AI Technology.

    f. The _____ as the name says is a new spin of 20 Questions Game.

    g. Identify the Mystery Animal game explains the _____ feature of AI in learning.

    h. Emoji Scavenger Hunt Game defines the use of _____ using the AI concept in our lives.

## CHAPTER 2

Applications of AI Towards Concept of Smart Cities

Definition of Smart Cities

Smart Cities are the cities which have digital technology embedded across all **city** functions.

A smart city is define as a developed urban area that creates sustainable economic development and high quality of life through human resources, social resources and ICT Infrastructure.

Smart city offers smart living which is about providing opportunities for a healthy lifestyle for all the citizens with special attention to their health care, education, safety and their security.

Objectives of Smart Cities include the following:

a. Provide basic infrastructure

b. Quality of life

c. Clean and sustainable environment

d. Application of smart solutions

Smart City Framework

A smart city framework has the following parts:

a. **Smart Infrastructure** – This deals with the physical buildings with digital insights of safety and comfort.

b. **Smart Governance** – The smart governance allows the use of internet and digital technology to create a progressive work environment.

c. **Smart Living** – This form of smart city allows a trend of improved standards in various aspects of day to day life with better and more balanced life with advice, tips and stories.

d. Smart Mobility – The smart mobility is a new way of thinking about how we get around clean, safe and efficient.

e. Smart Technology – This is one of the important frameworks of smart city format and activates monitoring and analysis of health, choices and living standards using the digital foot print.

f. Smart Economy – The term smart economy allows the new framework of business with the new understanding and approach towards the issues of growth, development and sustainability.

Use of Smart Cities

The Smart Cities offer the following advantages-

a. Smart living

b. Smart Environment

c. Smart Mobility

d. Smart Governance

e. Smart People

f. Smart Economy

Use of Technology in Smart Cities

The smart city uses the digital technology and ICT (Information and Communication Technologies) to improve the quality of living, work life and performance at all levels. This level of technology is helping better collection, processing and analysis of data through conventional and social media methods.

Need of Smart Cities

The smart cities are needed in order to enhance the performance and well being of its citizens, work towards reducing the costs and resource consumption and to let all the people engage effectively for the production process.

The smart cities are required to provide smart solutions like public data, electronic service delivery, 100% treatment of water waste, monitory water and air quality, climate awareness and control of pollution.

The smart cities also provide the following:

a. Development

b. Housing

c. Employment

d. Smart Economy

e. Smart Environment

f. Smart Living

g. Smart Governance

Our Prime Minister, Narendra Modi has a vision of developing 100 smart cities across the country.

Components of Smart Cities

The smart economy of a country provides a high level of work environment, high paying jobs, promotes innovation, productivity and efficiency through collaboration and team work.

The following are the components of smart cities:

a. Smart Governance

b. Smart Energy

c. Smart Building

d. Smart Mobility

e. Smart Infrastructure

f. Smart Technology

g. Smart Healthcare

h. Smart Citizen

i. Smart Environment

A smart city's objective is to protect our natural environment while planning for the future, it brings harmony and quality of work life and balances the energy supply and the usage.

We aim at living in a smart city to allow opportunities for everyone, recognizes the need for affordable housing, support to the aging population, culturally vibrant, promotes diversity and reaches out to every one to ensure inclusion.

It is an extension of a sustainable city and the objective is to create the most of the benefits for the people and making their life easier for all. It aims to deliver the best of the infrastructure, transport, power and the applications towards the welfare for all.

EXERCISE

1. Define the term SMART Cities.

2. Write about the objectives of Smart Cities.

3. What are the parts of a Smart City Framework?

4. What are the uses/advantages of Smart Cities?

5. Write about the use of Technology in Smart Cities.

6. What is the need of Smart Cities.

7. Name the various features offered by Smart Cities.

8. Name various components of Smart Cities.

9. Fill in the blanks:

   a. Smart Cities are the cities which have _____ embedded across all **city** functions.

   b. The _____ uses the digital technology and ICT (Information and Communication Technologies) to improve the quality of living.

   c. The smart cities are needed in order to _____the performance and well being of its citizens.

   d. The _____ _____ of a country provides a high level of work environment, high paying jobs, promotes innovation, productivity and efficiency through collaboration and team work.

   e. A smart city's objective is to protect our _____while planning for the future, it brings harmony and quality of work life and balances the energy supply and the usage.

10. Give the use of the following:

    a. Smart living

    b. Smart Environment

    c. Smart Mobility

    d. Smart Governance

    e. Smart People

    f. Smart Economy

## CHAPTER 3

Impact of AI on Sustainable Development Goals

The importance of AI as a technology framework has been made available for the development of the country. It is largely benefiting globally in the field of climate change and sustainable development.

Sustainable Development

The term sustainable development is the economic development of the nation without the depletion of its natural resources. The object of the sustainable development process is to satisfy the needs of today without compromising the needs of tomorrow.

We should not be using our resources and not leave anything for the future generation.

Use of AI In Sustainable Development

AI can support the achievement of various targets of development effectively. The various important fields where this may help a support include the Environment, Society and Economy.

AI will support low-carbon energy systems with high integration of renewable energy and energy efficiency which are needed to address the climate change. It also helps in identification of desertification and helps in environmental planning and decision making to avoid desertification and help driving model measures.

Objectives towards AI Implementation for sustainability

a. Towards Economy

b. Towards Society

c. Towards Environment

All the above three objectives adhere to the implementation of technology integrated with AI.

Role of AI to meet Economic Sustainability

a. Good health and well being

b. Quality Education

c. Responsible consumption and production

d. Climate Action

e. Life below water

f. Life on land

g. Industry innovation and infrastructure

h. Partnerships for the goals

AI Applications Supporting Sustainable Development

There are many effective AI Applications which support the sustainable development of the intelligent buildings and making them safe inclusive and resilient and sustainable.

AI drives business and innovation in areas where Artificial Intelligence is used as a promising tool for the sustainable development.

Some of the key applications of AI for this purpose are as follows:

a. Natural Language Processing

b. Speech Recognition

c. Computer Vision

d. Image Recognition

e. Data Analytics

f. Pattern Recognition

Sustainable Development Goals

In September 2015 the United Nations made history – 193 member states unanimously adopted the Sustainable Development Goals (SDGs).

These goals aim to economically develop the world in a way that eliminates poverty, respects planetary boundaries and leaves no one behind. The international community agreed that every country is responsible for achieving these goals, and that all members of society – governments, business, and civil society need to participate. world aspires to achieve by 2030.

The following are Sustainable Development Goals as per the United Nations which has been set as a road map to guarantee a sustainable future by 2030. These goals range from ending hunger and poverty over realizing sustainable energy and gender equality to preserving our biodiversity.

Three Dimensions of Sustainable Development

As per the United Nations the Sustainable development has been defined as development that meets the needs of the present without compromising the ability of future generations to meet their own needs. For sustainable development to be achieved, it is crucial to harmonize three core elements: **economic growth, social inclusion and environmental protection.**

The Five Ps:

This includes the following:

People

Prosperity

Peace

Partnership

Planet

The 17 Goals are as follows:

1. No Poverty

   End poverty in all its forms everywhere.

2. Zero Hunger

   End hunger, achieve food security and improved nutrition and promote sustainable agriculture.

3. Good Health & Well being

Ensure healthy lives and promote well-being for all at all ages.

4. Quality Education

Ensure inclusive and quality education for all and promote lifelong learning.

5. Gender Equality

Achieve gender equality and empower all women and girls.

6. Clean Water and Sanitation

This is to assure and ensure access to water and sanitation for all.

7. Affordable and clean energy

This is to ensure access to affordable, reliable, sustainable and modern energy for all.

8. Decent work and economic growth

   This is to promote inclusive and sustainable economic growth, employment and decent work for all.

9. Industry, Innovation and Infrastructure

   This is to build resilient infrastructure, promote sustainable industrialization and foster innovation.

10. Reduced Inequalities

    This is to reduce inequality within and among countries.

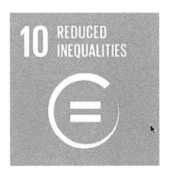

11. Sustainable Cities and Communities

This is to make the cities inclusive, safe, resilient and sustainable.

12. Responsible Consumption and Production

This is to ensure sustainable consumption and production patterns.

13. Climate Action

This is to take urgent action to combat climate change and its impacts.

14. Life Below Water

This is to conserve and sustainably use the oceans, seas and marine resources.

15. Life on Land

This refers to the sustainably management of forests, combat desertification, halt and reverse land degradation, halt biodiversity loss.

16. Peace, Justice and Strong Institutions

This is to promote just, peaceful and inclusive societies.

17. Partnership for the Goals

This is to revitalize the global partnership for the sustainable development.

How AI Can Help achieving the Sustainable Goals?

Goal #1: No Poverty

Tackling poverty is a universal concern. **Tackling poverty** in specific regions through improving farming lands and agriculture, increasing education and helping inhabitants learning new skills to support communities. **AI can** also help **with** aid distribution in poorer and war-torn areas, or where natural disasters have caused devastation. It goes a long way to explore the technological aspects in delivery.

Goal #2: Zero Hunger

The use of artificial intelligence in reducing hunger works with technology. Beyond recognising pictures of man's best friend, it has the power to transform the world we live and help provide a better, hunger free future. From enhanced communication interfaces that give us a better understanding of the people we help to automated transport and logistics systems, organisations are primed to take advantage of the technology to help us reach Zero Hunger faster. For the benefit of society, the use and development of AI must be balanced with a rights based approach; one that puts people's needs first.

Goal #3: Good Health & Well being

As per the sources, AI is promising to change the way workplaces operate, but will it be a force for good or disrupt workplace culture in negative ways? With the expectation that AI will create a $190.6 billion market by 2025, it could be a tool used to provide healthier, more productive, and accessible work environments for all employees.

Goal #4: Quality Education

The references quote the importance of quality in education and particularly, Using intelligent **AI**-powered systems tend to improve the efficiency of many **educational**

institutions, lower their operating costs, give them greater visibility into income and expenses, and improve the overall responsiveness of the **educational** institutions. As a matter of fact, **AI** is looking forward to automate the expedition of administrative duties for teachers and academic institutions. With the march of this invention, the Educators spend a lot of time on grading exams, assessing homework, and providing valuable responses to their students online with the advent of Artificial Intelligence and automation. Robots are replacing and assisting teachers in schools for the delivery of education and smart learning environment within classrooms.

Goal #5: Gender Equality

A report published by the AI Now Institute in April 2019 found that only 18% of authors at leading AI conferences are women and more than 80% of professors in the field are men. At market-leading companies, the situation is even more confronting. Only 15% of AI researchers at Facebook and 10% of AI researchers at Google are women. It is expected that using Artificial Intelligence, we need to understand and confront the gender bias. The field of artificial intelligence (AI) is growing at a rapid pace, developing algorithms and automated machines that show promise in making the workplace **more efficient and less biased**. AI hiring and talent-management systems have the potential to **move the needle on gender equality in workplaces by using more objective criteria in recruiting and promoting talent**.

Goal #6: Clean Water and Sanitation

To achieve SDG6 and ensure the access to and sustainable management of water and sanitation, AI can also play a fundamental role to manage water resources and change the way water utilities operate. Water is at the heart of sustainable development and its three dimensions — environmental, economic and social. AnyTech is a Tokyo-based company established in 2015 that has been turning heads for its innovative approach to clean water. It's using computer vision and deep learning, an approach to

AI, to automatically detect contaminants in water. The technology is quicker and cheaper than traditional methods and could be a game-changer for the sanitation industry.

Goal #7: Affordable and clean energy

While the biggest goal of AI in renewable energy is to manage the intermittency, it can also offer improved safety, efficiency, and reliability.

It can help you understand the energy consumption patterns, identify the energy leakage and health of the devices.

For example, the AI-powered predictive analysis can collect the data from wind turbine sensors to monitor wear and tear. The system will monitor the overall health of the equipment and alert the operator when the maintenance is needed.

Goal #8: Decent work and economic growth

AI technologies will be used to reducing need for human work on monotonous and dangerous work such as mining, repetitive factory and agricultural work and dangerous industrial work. The pace of this change is faster than it has ever been in history and importantly, the pace is now *sub-generational*. This means that entire career paths are becoming obsolete or changing beyond recognition well within one worker's lifetime. Retraining and education are pivotal efforts to move forward but they may not be enough to navigate the next 50 years in a humane way. When these technologies are generating such wealth and efficiency it is unavoidable that this wealth be used to move societies towards a humane and fair new type of economy where the value of a citizen is more than the sum of their wages.

Goal #9: Industry, Innovation and Infrastructure

Artificial Intelligence promises support to the people in various industries, ranging from technology to health care, to marketing, to sales, to legal about value adding through innovation and competency. It is being used to add quality and perfection value and growth above all to data processing and industry workflows explores the complex reasoning and data analysis.

It is exploring the image recognition, reality modelling and natural language processing to get the productivity at scale in particular. The reality modelling applications using the deep learning can be used to overcome many industry challenges, making it possible for computer vision and image recognition to identify problems with structures or individual pieces of equipment before they become critical.

Goal #10: Reduced Inequalities

As per the available data: "In terms of *AI*, the inclusion policy must therefore take on a double objective: ensure that the development of these technologies does not contribute to increase social and economic *inequalities*; and *use AI* to effectively *reduce* these."

A major objective, as in this area things are not straightforward. Contributing to this effectiveness and salute to this, Microsoft's Seeing AI and Google's Lookout applications help blind or visually impaired people to identify elements (individuals, objects, text, etc.) present in their surroundings, thanks to automatic image recognition. And beyond this, AI has a great potential to simplify uses in the digital world and thus narrow the digital divide.

Goal #11: Sustainable Cities and Communities

The emergence of artificial intelligence (AI) and its progressively wider impact on many sectors across the society requires an assessment of its effect on sustainable development. A wide range of new technologies are being developed very fast, significantly affecting the way individuals live, requiring new piloting procedures from governments. Examples of the positive impacts include AI algorithms aimed at improving fraud detection. Technology is changing society. Digitization is challenging the way we live. These changes create conveniences and ways of problem-solving that were never possible before.

Goal #12: Responsible Consumption and Production

The Artificial Intelligence is now offering an increasingly quantified society. By gathering data about our preferences, browsing history and more other people have power over us. They know what makes us tick and they know our "carrots" and "sticks." In the example of Cambridge Analytica and the 2016 U.S. presidential campaign, the company had a couple of thousand data points about 200 million Americans. This enabled them to project an image of a candidate that was tailored to the preferences and prejudices and biases at an individual level. AI is yielding optimal consumption and production levels with vertical green farms, eliminating waste and vastly improving yields and resource efficiency. It is encapsulating meaningful solution to the catch for global cyberthreats, the Cyber kill chain, in a manner which was not possible before. Responsible AI is concerned about fairness and equality of gender, race or similar protected attributes.

Goal #13: Climate Action

The AI – Artificial Intelligence is a game changer for climate change and the environment. In India, AI has helped farmers get 30 percent higher groundnut yields per hectare by providing information on preparing the land, applying fertilizer and choosing sowing dates. In Norway, AI helped create a flexible and autonomous electric grid, integrating more renewable energy. Microsoft believes that AI is a game changer for climate change and environmental issues. The company's AI for Earth program has committed $50 million over five years to create and test new applications for AI. Eventually it will help scale up and commercialize the most promising projects. Another project, named Protection Assistant for Wildlife Security (PAWS) from the University of Southern California, is using machine learning to predict where poaching may occur in the future. Currently the algorithm analyses past ranger patrols and poachers' behaviour from crime data; a Microsoft grant will help train it to incorporate real time data to enable rangers to improve their patrols.

Goal #14: Life Below Water

The use of Artificial Intelligence empowers new advances in satellite observation, open data and machine learning to track and measure life under water. It makes the conservation and sustainability of life below water. As we know the humans have polluted the oceans to dangerous levels with offshore drilling, cargo transport, and trash – one garbage truck of plastic is dumped into the oceans every minute, amounting to eight million metric tons of plastic annually. But AI is already coming to the rescue: the first effort expected to effectively start deconstructing the Great Pacific Garbage Patch is essentially an autonomous floating garbage truck powered by AI. In other oceans, machine learning is making it possible to follow marine litter in real-time, enabling responses that are quick, targeted, and more effective. The monitoring and predictive technology of machine learning can also help researchers understand the human actions and subsequent changing conditions that harm the oceans, such as coral bleaching, illegal fishing, disease outbreak and industrial activity in particular.

Goal #15: Life on Land

As a matter of fact and to the surprise of all, the Artificial Intelligence power has the capacity to completely transform agricultural practices to make them safe for the Earth and people's health. Machine learning combined with robotics can provide automated data collection and decision-making to optimize farming processes. These systems can interact directly with crops to detect and act on the best times to plant, spray and harvest, decreasing the need for the fertilizers and pesticides polluting the soil. This will make farming not only efficient, but it will also lead to more organic earth friendly crops. Similarly, AI monitoring can help societies protect areas of land larger than just farms; ecosystems and habitats all over the world can benefit as well. AI enabled drones, are providing new opportunities to observe and protect endangered areas. More effective plant disease detection, poacher route prediction, erosion monitoring, species identification and animal migration tracking are all a reality with AI, according to the World Economic report.

Goal #16: Peace, Justice and Strong Institutions

The leaders like, Ibaraki believe that, thoughtful application of **AI** can reduce discrimination and corruption and drive broad access to e-government, personalized and responsive intelligent services. **AI** can significantly stay ahead of global cyber threats in a manner not possible before, According to the United Nations Development Programme (UNDP), the Artificial Intelligence shall prove to be as robots to be used for the Peace, Justice and Strong Institutions. It shall wider the impact on these sectors across the society and shall support the achievement of 128 targets across all Sustainable Development Goals. It offers development through Peace, justice and strong institutions in particular.

Goal #17: Partnership for the Goals

AI is expected to affect global productivity, equality and inclusion, environmental outcomes and several other areas, both in the short and the long term. The objective is entirely to become one of the partners for good. As per the reports, AI will spur global growth more than earlier innovations like steam power. It is going to help the various goals. The contribution has been made active with the introduction of the AI Initiatives via data analysis and image recognition features in particular. The help is being provided to various countries to develop policies, leadership skills, patnering abilities, institutional capabilities of partnership and business outcomes. It also aims at transforming the use of technology to support the delivery of the SDGs. To add to the wisdom, a community has been forming, with the AI for Good Global Summit in Geneva as the annual synchronization among efforts. AI Commons, a new initiative and organisation dedicated to problem solving with AI more democratic and accessible; and a framework for the coordination of scaling of AI for Good.

Hence AI has great promise to help solve the SDGs and spread the opportunities and benefits of AI to all of civilization, for everyone.

EXERCISE

1. What do you mean by the term Sustainable Development Goals?

2. Write about the uses of AI in attaining the SDG.

3. What are the objectives of AI Implementation for Sustainability.

4. Mention the various fields where AI helps in meeting the economic sustainability.

5. Write about the various applications of AI for the purpose of supporting Sustainable Development.

6. Name the various sustainable development goals as per the UN.

7. Fill in the blanks:

   a. The term _____ is the economic development of the nation without the depletion of its natural resources.

   b. The three objectives towards AI implementation for sustainability are _____, _____ and _____.

   c. AI drives business and innovation in areas where Artificial Intelligence is used as a promising tool for the _____.

   d. The Sustainable Development Goals as the UN has been set as a road map to guarantee a sustainable future by _____.

   e. There are _____ Goals set by the UN.

## CHAPTER 4

Applications of AI

We have come across very innovative applications of AI in our lives. With the launch of the technology and its advancement on a fast manner, the AI has targeted its penetration in nearly every sphere.

Some of the following applications of AI include:

a. AI – Assisted Robotic Surgery

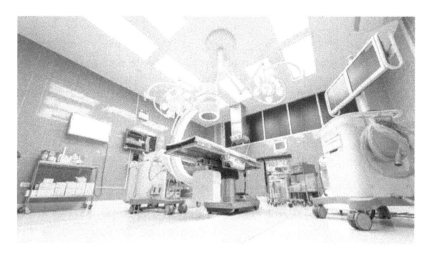

The AI assisted Robotic surgery is no longer seen as a technology of the future – it's an active and effective technology of today controlled well by the surgeon actively.

b. Intelligent Automation

The Intelligent Automation is one of the effective applications of AI in business processes and allows complex decision making simpler and faster.

c. Robotic Process Automation

Here the AI performs the work with learning capabilities to handle high volumes and repeatable tasks which were earlier done by the humans. The assignments includes queries, calculations and maintenance of records and operations.

d. Natural Language Processing

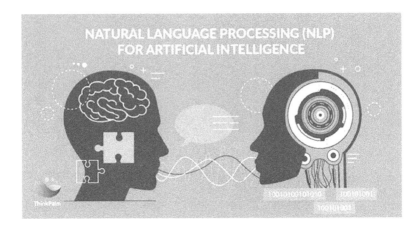

It is the application of computational techniques to do the analysis and the synthesis of Natural Language and speech. It allows easy interactions between the humans and the computers. It allows the computers to understand the human language as it is spoken.

e. Video Analytics

This is one such application of AI which tracks the moving image with the help of a sophisticated IP Camera. It has the capability of automatically analysing video to detect and determine events.

f. Biometrics

This is one of the applications which relate towards biometric recognition of people for security applications and identity verification or identification purposes.

It is able to inspect and store the person's face, iris, DNA, Vein, fingerprints for recognition.

g. Cognitive Robotics

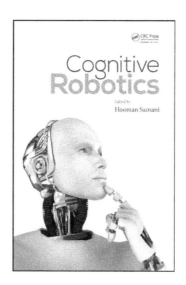

This is one such applications which relates to a robot with an intelligent behaviour by providing it with skills which include learning from experience, from humans and even on their own in order to deal effectively with the environment.

The objective is to let the robots act and react well at the real life scenarios.

h. Facial Recognition

This is one of the applications to recognize a human face through technology. We have this facility in our mobile phones where the facial recognition is done through biometrics to map the facial features through a photograph or a video.

i. Mini Robots/Virtual Assistants/Chatbots

It is one of the applications which relate to virtual assistants and communication tools through AI.

Here the real-time support is provided by the virtual assistance with AI Intelligence and are widely in use for the banks websites and other work areas.

j. Expert Systems

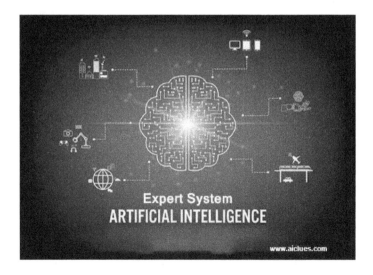

As the word says, expert systems, it is the application which provides the decision-making ability of a human expert in order to solve complex problems by reasoning through knowledge and cognitive computing.

k. Machine Learning

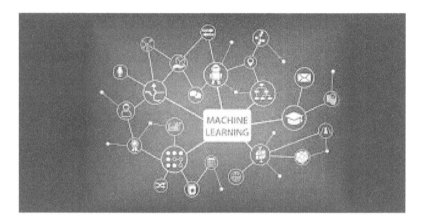

It is an application of Artificial Intelligence which provides the computers the ability to automatically learning and improve from experience without any explicit programming. This feature allows the computer to access data and learn by itself in making decisions.

l. Gesture Recognition

This application of Artificial Intelligence allows computers to capture and act towards human gestures as commands.

These gestures are normally from the face and hands. The concept used is deep learning and computer vision techniques. Some of the examples may include the Facial Recognition in Mobiles, Voice Recognition, eye tracking and lip movement.

m. Computer Vision

This application is also known as Image Processing and is used to emulate the vision at a human scale.

Here the computer is able to acquire, process, analyse and understand the digital images from the real world and interpret towards meaningful information.

n. Deep Learning

The term deep learning is a broader family of machine learning and it is used for performing operations which typically require the human intelligence. It allows the computers to solve complex problems even when using a data set that is diverse, unstructured and inter connected.

The common examples include the Virtual Assistants and Chat Bots, Translations, Vision for driverless cars, Facial Recognition and personalised shopping and entertainments (Netflix) among others.

o. Neural Networks

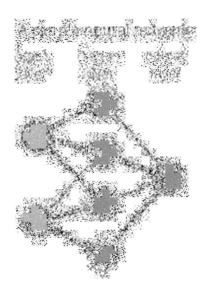

The Neural Networks relate to the applications like Speech Recognition, Character Recognition, Spell Checking, Machine Translation among others. It allows modelling of non linear proesses.

Domains of AI

The various domains of AI include:

    a. Machine Learning

    b. NLP

    c. Knowledge Base

    d. Deep Learning

    e. Computer Vision

    f. Expert Systems

EXERCISE

1. Name the various applications of AI
2. Write about the following in brief:
   a. The AI Assisted Robotic Surgery
   b. Intelligent Automation
   c. Natural Language Processing
   d. Biometrics
   e. Video Analytics
3. What are expert systems?
4. Explain the use of Mini Robots/Virtual Assistants/Chatbots.
5. What is the application of Machine Learning.
6. Define the use of Gesture Recognition.
7. How does Computer Vision help in AI.
8. Explain the term Deep Learning.
9. What are Neural Networks.

10. Fill in the blanks:

    a. The _____ is no longer seen as a technology of the future – it's an active and effective technology of today controlled well by the surgeon actively.

    b. The _____ is one of the effective applications of AI in business processes and allows complex decision making simpler and faster.

    c. In Robotic Process Automation AI performs the work with _____ to handle high volumes and repeatable tasks which were earlier done by the humans.

    d. _____ allows easy interactions between the humans and the computers. It allows the computers to understand the human language as it is spoken.

    e. Cognitive Robotics is one such applications which relates to _____by providing it with skills which include learning from experience, from humans and even on their own in order to deal effectively with the environment.

11. Explain the following terms:

    a. Machine Learning

    b. Gesture Recognition

    c. Computer Vision

    d. Deep Learning

    e. Neural Networks

    f. Facial Recognition

12. Name the various domains of AI.

## CHAPTER 5

Ethical Issues Around AI

AI Ethics – Definition

The Term AI – Ethics represents the part of regulations of the use of technology related to the robots and other artificial intelligent machines. It is mandatory of the fact that the use of technology integrated with AI should be used and matched with utmost care and concern keeping the view of the human interactions as safe and comfortable.

The objective has to be to gain awareness around AI bias and AI access and let students analyse the advantages and disadvantages of Artificial Intelligence.

Importance of AI Ethics

The very purpose of AI Ethics is to make aware and prepare the stakeholders when engaged with an AI based device. Also to reflect and understand on the ethical issues around AI.

There are instances where the use of AI is causing fear of disruptive, confusing, offensive and even dangerous. A recent incident in San Francisco ended up in banning the law department from using the FACIAL RECOGNITION Technology.

There are debates and discussions on about the unrestrained use of AI giving pace to challenging the democratic rights and individual freedom of the people.

Referring to the news report at venturebeat.com:

A study of 1,010 UK tech workers found that 90 percent consider technology a force for good, but 59 percent of those working in AI said they had worked on projects they felt might be harmful to society; 18 percent quite their jobs over ethical concerns.

Types of AI Ethics

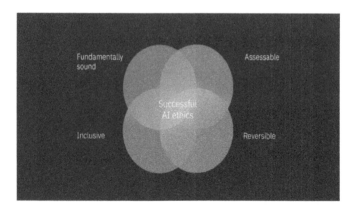

AI Ethics include the following context towards moral behaviour of human like intelligent machines with human beings.

   a. Robot Ethics – This means the rules should be listed for robots to ensure their ethical behaviour and protect humans from their design.

b. Biases in AI Systems – The misuse of data in applying AI can develop implicit racial, gender or ideological governments to businesses. There has to be a trust between humans and machines.

c. Liability for Automated Cars – The liability for incidents involving self-driving cars with the primary motivation of reducing the frequency of road accidents.

d. Weaponization of AI – The debate is on towards the speculation about the power and the dangers of AI in warfare or otherwise it seems like a scary match for the society.

e. Machine Ethics – This defines the moral behaviour of the artificially intelligent machines.

f. Human Dignity – When human dignity meets Artificial Intelligence we have ethical questions to answer. The question is whether AI be considered a person under the law?

Asimov's 3 Laws of Robotics

Issac Asimov is the first person to use the term ROBOTICS in his short story written in 1940s. He devised three golden principles to guide the conduct of robots and intelligent machines.

These principles or laws relate as follows:

a. *Robots must never harm human beings or, through inaction, allow a human being to come to harm.*

b. *Robots must follow instructions from humans without violating rule 1.*

c. *Robots must protect themselves without violating the other rules.*

Measures by the Government to Control Right Usage of AI

Canada's Directive on Automated Decision-Making offers a leading model for governments looking to create a framework for transparent AI. Using a tool called Algorithmic Impact Assessment (AIA), the Canadian government has created a process for the use of AI in both the public and private sectors.

Source: Venturebeat.com

EXERCISE

1. What do you mean by AI Ethics?

2. What is AI Ethics so important?

3. How AI can be dangerous?

4. Name the various types of AI Ethics.

5. Explain the Asimov's 3 Laws of Robotics.

6. Who was Issac Asimov and what did he do for Robotics.

7. Explain the following terms:

   a. AAI

   b. Human Dignity

   c. Machine Ethics

   d. Weaponization of AI

   e. Robot Ethics

8. Fill in the blanks:

   a. The very purpose of AI Ethics is to make aware and prepare the stakeholders when engaged with an _____.

   b. The Term AI – Ethics represents the part of regulations of the use of _____related to the robots and other artificial intelligent machines.

   c. There are debates and discussions on about the _____ use of AI giving pace to challenging the democratic rights and individual freedom of the people.

   d. Machine Ethics defines the moral behaviour of the _____ machines.

CHAPTER 6

AI Project Cycle

(Problem Scoping, Data Acquisition, Data Exploration and Modelling)

Project Management of AI

It is a system that can execute the day to day activities of the management and administration of projects without requiring the human input. It is expected to develop the understanding of the key projects.

The AI is a field of Computer Science which is dedicated to solving problems which otherwise require human intelligence – like that of pattern recognition, learning and generalization.

As per the project management practice of AI, Data is the King. As per the BCG report, many companies do not understand the importance of data and training to AI success but better data is more crucial to building of an intelligent system which can offer weightage over human beings.

The Project cycle mainly involves the preparing and cleaning data. The data preparation is a key step in AI project Management.

The main functions include:

a. Learning – This is fetching the information.

b. Pattern Detection – Gaining the recognition pattern or the format.

c. Data – Facts/Figures or information.

d. Self Programming – Auto instructions format.

The AI Development Lifecycle

The AI Development Lifecycle has the following steps:

    a. Ideation and Data discovery

    b. Prioritizing the minimum viable product (MVP)

    c. MVP to full-fledged product

Skills Required in AI Field:

    Data Scientists

    Data Engineer

    Infrastructure Engineer

The most common challenges acquired by AI today include the following:

    a. Reality Check

    b. AI Scope Creep

    c. Quality Assurance and Testing Practices

    d. Theft and Plagiarism

    e. Talent Shortages

    f. Legal and Ethical Challenges

Ai Project Cycle

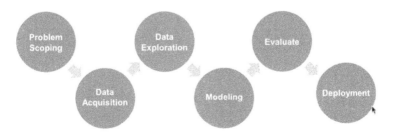

(Problem Scoping, Data Acquisition, Data Exploration and Modelling)

Problem Scoping in AI

The term problem scoping relates to the selection of the problem which has to be solved using the power of Artificial Intelligence. It helps to Enquire about and state the problem for the project cycle and create a system map.

Take in consideration about the world's largest building, is in danger and a person named ROBIN has threatened to blow it. No one is able to track Mr. Robin and hence the situation is critical. Say, Mr. X has been appointed as the Chief Officer to enhance the security of the building. Mr. X plans to implement the AI to assure the safety of the building.

Some of the factors which Mr. X would be needing for the security mechanism would be the following:

a. Problem Scoping

b. Data Acquisition

c. Data Exploration

d. Modelling

Here the Problem Scoping is actually the nature of the problem or the project to be solved.

Note for Teachers

Ensure that continuity is maintained in mentorship and monitoring to facilitate students' learning. Online feedback, Interactive discussions on problems and challenges are some of the ways to assist this.

Activity of Problem Scoping

Learning Objectives:

• Apply the problem scoping framework

• Frame a Goal for the project

Session Preparation:

Logistics: For a class of 40 Students

Purpose:

Understanding how to narrow down to a problem statement from a broad theme.

Teachers' Quote:

"Let us now start with the first stage of AI Project Cycle that is – Problem scoping! As we have understood, Problem Scoping means selecting a problem which we might want to solve using our AI knowledge.

Brief:

Students will be selecting a theme either out of those mentioned in the handbook or from anywhere outside. They will then look inside the theme and find out topics where problems exist. They need to understand the vastness of a theme because of which one needs to go deeper. After listing down the topics, they will then find out various problems which exist under them. These problems will now be very specific as they have been narrowed down from a broader perspective. Ask the students to select any one problem out of the ones they scoped and write it as the goal of their project. Doing this, gives them a clear vision as to what exactly are they looking forward to solve using their AI knowledge.

Scoping of the problem may be done through the selection from the following themes which may interest you:

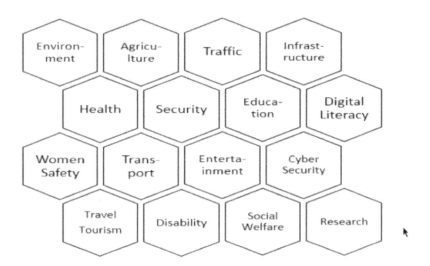

Accordingly select the theme and the problem as per the following format:

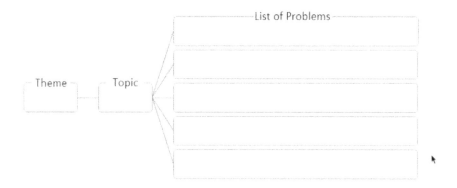

Considering the above case:

Take in consideration about the world's largest building, is in danger and a person named ROBIN has threatened to blow it. No one is able to track Mr. Robin and hence the situation is critical. Say, Mr. X has been appointed as the Chief Officer to enhance the security of the building. Mr. X plans to implement the AI to assure the safety of the building.

Note for Teachers:

Facilitating and Feedback Learning to Facilitate is learning to know the difference between when to guide/suggest and when to allow students to figure out and understand for themselves, question, hypothesize and take the challenge. Being a Facilitator is mostly about how to motivate, encourage and simplify. Learning to use appropriate vocabulary while giving feedback is the skill set most required by a Facilitator. Give feedback in a positive manner to inspire students to explore and persevere in their learning.

Data Acquisition in AI

The data acquisition refers to the collection of data for the needful project. Referred to as DAQ, it is done using the 4Ws problem canvas for Who/What/Where and Why.

Who?

This helps you to analyse the people getting affected. The word stakeholders applies to this category.

What?

This relates to what we have in hand. Here we need to determine the nature of the project or the assignment. What is the assignment and how do we about it. Here we gather the evidence to prove that the assignment or the problem we have selected actually is in real.

Where?

This replicates about the location of the assignment or the location of the concern in particular. This helps us to know about the situation in which the problem arises and comes in place of its being the most.

Why?

This may be one of the most important elements that may affect the concern. The above canvas help us in understanding the concern the better. The 'why' canvas allows us to replicate about the benefits which the stakeholders would get from the solution derived and how it may value them in particular.

Keeping the above project in view, Mr. X has to track the whereabout of Mr. Robin who threatened to blow the building.

A data has to be acquired of the current situation of the building, like, collecting the photographs, accuracy, area, safety precautions. This is Acquisition of Data.

The collected data is further classified as:

a. Historical Data

b. Testing Data

If you miss the details and insert the wrong data flagged as pipe which is not, then the code will be weak AI.

If you take care of the training data set carefully and have its domain set to big data set. AI will be Strong AI.

To achieve better solutions for the clients we need fast and more accurate approach, and that includes AI, but without quality data AI will not work better. It will become full of ambiguities.

After filling the 4Ws' problem canvas, we now need to summarise all the cards into one template to be named as the Problem Statement Template. It further helps in summarising the key points into one single template to depict the key elements clearly.

Data Exploration in AI

Now keeping the above acquired data using Data Acquisition process, Mr. X, the security officer shall be interpreting the data, evaluating the facts and information, do analysis and this is known as Data Exploration in AI.

Data Visualisation is one of the steps involved in this process. It is the creation of a mental image through charts, process, diagrams or pictures. This helps in comprehending the trends and patterns to present in data to decide the strategies and the course of action of the AI cycle in particular. It encompasses the data analysis and helps in identifying the patterns to implement the course of action.

Note for Teachers

Preparatory Groundwork Reading and gathering all information one can get about what is AI and what is not – is imperative for a better understanding of the subject. Be prepared to connect to new learning on the basis of your previous knowledge. – Read, Research, inquire, ask questions, watch videos, talk for and against AI, walk through Malls, airports, hospitals and try to figure out what is AI and what is not.

The data visualisation is depicted at the following website:

https://datavizcatalogue.com/

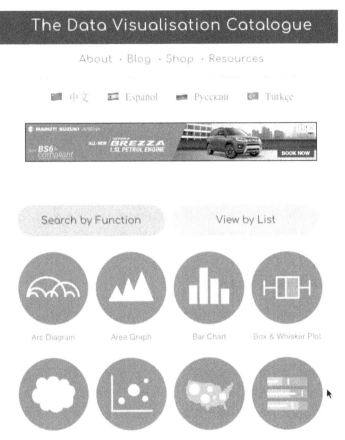

The website showcases the various types of Data Visualisation techniques which can be used to depict the data. The images are clear for the various data representation format with various charts used for both analysis and the communication required. This may feature as relationships, processes, methods. They include the data visualization techniques as Bar Graph, Histogram, Pie Chart, Line Graph and many more.

Activity for Students

Kindly explore the Data Visualization catalogue at https:// datavizcatalogue.com/ to understand the various techniques. Categorize any three techniques as a description, example and the purpose as a project activity in your exercise books.

Visualisation Tools:

In addition to the depiction, the tools used for this technique are as follows:

a. MS Excel

b. Apple Numbers

c. Google Charts

d. Google Docs

e. OnlineChartTool.com

f. Python Graph Gallery

Data Modelling in AI

Once the data exploration is over, it is time to implement the logic and the idea to execute some planning using the algorithms and implement computer vision approach of AI. This is known as Modelling stage of the AI Project Cycle. The idea is to go through various models and select the one which matches the requirement and is implemented.

Students will be introduced to rule based and AI models and undertake activities to appreciate the distinction between each. They will receive an overview of the various types of regression, classification and clustering models.

Modelling refers to developing algorithms which is designed towards the effectiveness, efficiency and reliability.

AI supports two types of models:

a. Learning Approach

The Learning Based Approach is the path through which the machine learns through experience. The models and algorithms assist the mechanism. Sample data is the base used as the training data. In this process the coder need not direct what to do, instead the instructions are fed in with the data where a comparison is done with the previous data through learning.

b. Rule Based Approach

The Rule Based System is used to store and manipulate knowledge to interpret information in a useful way. They are often used in AI and research. It is applied to systems involving human-crafted or curated rule sets. It focuses on representing the knowledge in a useful manner. They can solve a wide range of potentially complex problems by selecting relevant rules and then combining the results. It determines the best sequence of rules to examine. Here in the Rule based approach, the machine follows the rules or instructions mentioned by the developer, and performs its task accordingly.

For example, suppose you have a dataset comprising of 100 images of oranges and 100 images of bananas. To train your machine, you feed this data into the machine and label each image as either an orange or a banana. Now if you test the machine with the image of an orange, it will compare the image with the trained data and according to the labels of trained images, it will identify the test image as an orange. This is known as Rule based approach.

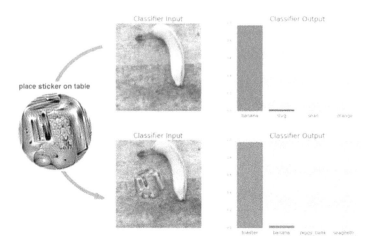

Image Courtesy: https://techcrunch.com/2018/01/02/these-psychedelic-stickers-blow-ai-minds/

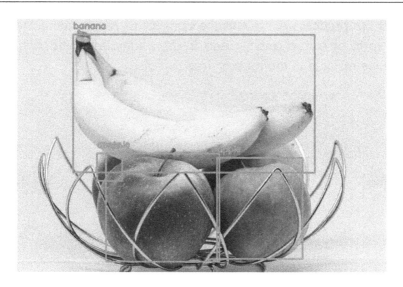

Learning via Modelling:

1. Learning AI process

2. Rule based vs AI model

3. Decision Trees

4. Image Classification

The rule based approach uses the rules as the knowledge representation. The most important objective is to capture the knowledge of a human expert in a specialized domain and embody it within a computer system. The knowledge here is encoded as rules in particular.

Decision Tree:

The Decision Tree represents a rule-based AI model which supports the machine in predicting what an element is with the help of various decisions or rules which are given into it.

As per the CBSE Resource Manual:

Decision Trees are similar to the concept of Story Speaker. It is a rule-based AI model which helps the machine in predicting what an element is with the help of various decisions (or rules) fed to it.

It is the process which uses the concept of representing the data in the form of a tree and is used in the examples of classifications where the result is in the form of True or False.

It has the following components:

Root:

A root is the starting point of any decision tree.

Branches:

The branches offer conditions.

Leaf:

The leaf represents the decision.

And hence it is known as a decision tree!

Each node in the tree is the case which branches out to another case or corresponds to one of the possible answers.

A basic structure of the decision tree is shown below:

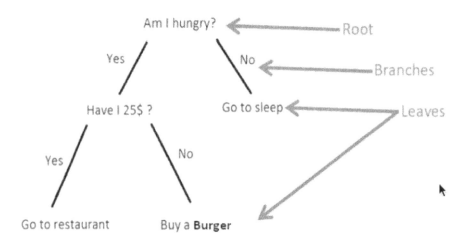

Here, the decision tree starts from the question Am I hungry?

The beginning point of any Decision Tree is known as its Root.

It then forks into two different ways or conditions. Yes or No.

The forks or diversions are known as Branches of the tree. The branches either lead to another question, or they lead to a decision like Go To Sleep which is known as the leaf. If you look closely at the image above, you would notice that it looks like an inverted tree with root above and the leaves below. The leaves are the decisions or the final outcomes. Hence the name Decision Tree!

Let's illustrate this with an example:

Assume we want to play badminton on a Sunday.

How will you decide whether to play or not? Let us check the weather, temperature, humidity and wind.

Weather: Sunny/Cloudy/Rainy

Temperature: Hot/Mild/Cool

Humidity: High/Normal

Wind: Weak/Strong

A decision tree for the above may be as follows:

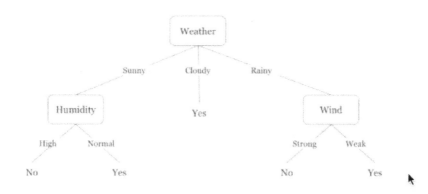

As a matter of fact, the decision trees made on the basis of the dataset we have can change according to the parameters for modelling. We need to visualise the relation amongst all the parameters given to formulate an ideal model in particular.

Points to remember:

- While making Decision Trees, one should take a good look at the data given and consider the parameters for the output leaf to follow.

- We should ignore the redundant data while creating a decision tree which at times may club during the formation.

- We must consider the simplest Decision Tree for a given condition out of multiple formats available.

Do it Yourself!

Play Football!!

The following is a dataset comprising of 4 parameters which lead to the prediction of whether it is ideal to play football or not?

The parameters which effect prediction are:

Outlook, Temperature, Humidity and wind. Draw the Decision Tree for this dataset.

Outlook: Sunny/Overcast/Rain

Temperature: Hot/Mild/Cold

Humidity: High/Normal

Wind: Weak/Strong

Ideal to Play Football? Y/N

As per the AI Curriculum book of the CBSE

In order to understand Modelling, it Is wiser to get to know about the three terms AI, ML and DL.

Purpose:

To differentiate between Artificial Intelligence (AI), Machine Learning (ML) and Deep Learning (DL).

Say: "As we enter the world of modelling, it is a good time to clarify something many of you may be having doubts about. You may have heard the terms AI, ML and DL when research content online and during this course. They are of course related, but how? Artificial Intelligence, or AI for short, refers to any technique that enables computers to mimic human intelligence. An artificially intelligent machine works on algorithms and data fed to it and gives the desired output. Machine Learning, or ML for short, enables machines to improve at tasks with experience.

The machine here learns from the new data fed to it while testing and uses it for the next iteration. It also takes into account the times when it went wrong and considers the exceptions too. Deep Learning, or DL for short, enables software to train itself to perform tasks with vast amounts of data. Since the system has got huge set of data, it is able to train itself with the help of multiple machine learning algorithms working altogether to perform a specific task. Artificial Intelligence is the umbrella term which holds both Deep Learning as well as Machine Learning. Deep Learning, on the other hand, is the very specific learning approach which is a subset of Machine Learning as it comprises of multiple Machine Learning algorithms."

PIXEL IT!

This is another type of AI Modelling where we explore the computerised classification of images and their processing. It uses the concept of computer vision.

We shall understand this model through an activity:

Purpose:

To know how the computer classifies images as well as how the computer reads them.

Here the machine learning approach is being used.

Activity:

- Cut out the matrix from the page given below or draw the same on a blank page with 6x6 square blocks.

- Write an upper alphabet on this matrix. The height of the alphabet should be equal to the height of this matrix. In other words, it should start from the bottom line of the matrix till the top line. You can write any capital alphabet in any handwriting.

- Now colour the boxes on which the lines of that alphabet have fallen.

- After this, cut out horizontal stripes of the matrix such that it goes from 1–2, 2–3, 3–4, 4–5, 5–6 and 6–7.

- Now, paste all these stripes together to form a single paper string. Make sure that the last block should neither be over the first block of next line or should there be any gap in between the first and the last blocks.

- Now, find those students in your class who have chosen the same alphabet as you. Put their paper strings under your string and add up all the coloured blocks to get a series of numbers. A block without colour counts as 0 while the coloured ones count as 1. If a column has 3 coloured boxes, the summation turns out to be 3.

- Now, get another student whose letter is different from yours. Put his paper string under your multiple strings (of same alphabet) and see if the pattern of coloured blocks is the same or not.

- Also, go to other groups and check if their summation series of numbers is the same as yours or not.

- Note down your observations in the end.

1						2
2						3
3						4
4						5
5						6
6						7

Cut out this matrix

Write an uppercase alphabet on this matrix. The height of the alphabet should be equal to the height of this matrix. In other words, it should start from the bottom line of the matrix till the top line. You can write any capital alphabet in any handwriting.

Like below:

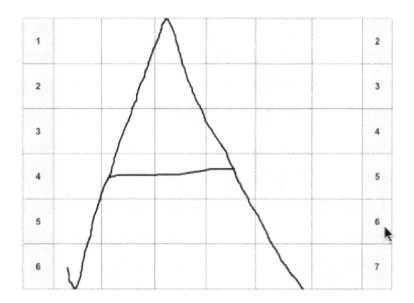

Now color the boxes on which the lines of that alphabet has fallen as below:

Now cut out the horizontal stripes of the matrix such that it goes from 1–2, 2–3, 3–4, 4–5, 5–6 and 6–7 as follows:

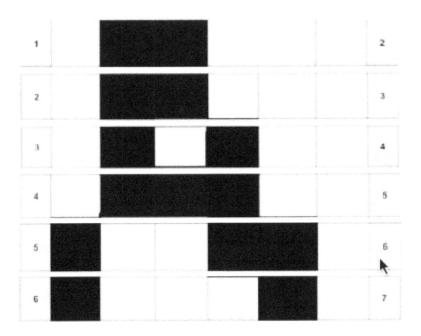

Paste all these stripes together to form a single paper string. Make sure that the last block should neither be over the first block of next line nor should there be any gap in between the first and the last blocks.

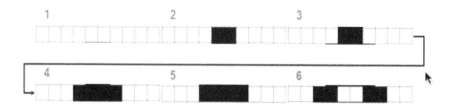

Now find those students in your class who have chosen the same alphabet as you. Put their stings under your string and do the addition of all the coloured blocks to get a series of numbers. Blocks without colour count as 0 while the coloured ones count as 1, If a column has 3 coloured boxes, the summation turns out to be 3.

0341001430

Follow the rest of the steps to finish the activity.

Our learning:

This activity is an example of Image Recognition. How computers look at images, process them and classify them. Likewise, every image which is fed to the computer is divided into pixels, being the smallest unit of an image. Each pixel is analysed by the computer.

The CBSE Curriculum Further Defines

Modelling and its Purpose: (Re-visited)

Classification of Models into Rule-based approach and Learning approach.

Say: "In general, there are two approaches taken by researchers when building AI models. They either take a rule based approach or learning approach. A Rule based approach is generally based on the data and rules fed to the machine, where the machine reacts accordingly to deliver the desired output. Under learning approach, the machine is fed with data and the desired output to which the machine designs its own algorithm (or set of rules) to match the data to the desired output fed into the machine"

AI Modelling refers to developing algorithms, also called models which can be trained to get intelligent outputs. That is, writing codes to make a machine artificially intelligent. Let us ponder Use your knowledge and thinking ability and answer the following questions:

1. What makes a machine intelligent?

2. How can a machine be Artificially Intelligent?

3. Can Artificial Intelligence be a threat to Human Intelligence? How?

Hence we conclude of the following fact:

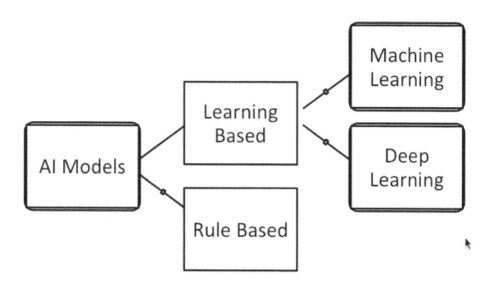

Other AI Models:
(Source: CBSE Academic Manual)

a. Regression

This type of Rule Based AI model is based on generating algorithms using a mapping function from the given data and is represented by a solid line. Here the dots represent the data values and the line represents the mapping done for them. With the help of this mapping function, we can predict the future data. Say for example, we need to predict the consumption of electricity by a house hold, we can use the past readings of the household consumption as training data and can predict the next consumption value. Regression works with continuous data.

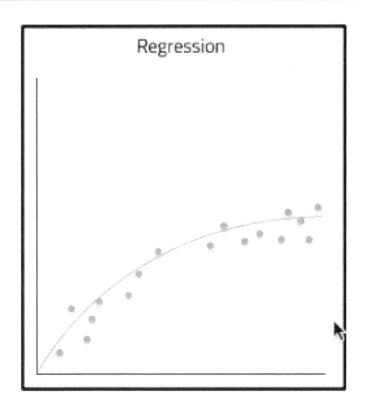

b. Classification

The classification is yet another Rule Based AI Model. Here the algorithm is able to determine which set of a given data point belongs to by means of a classification function represented by the dotted line. The model classifies data sets according to the rules given to it. These data sets are labelled and are sorted according to their labelling. The testing data is then classified as one of the labels of the training data set. Say for example, we need to train a model to identify if an image is of a hockey stick or a cricket bat, we need to train it with multiple images of both hockey stick and cricket bat along with their labels. The machine will then classify images on the basis of the labels and predict the correct label for testing data. Classification works on discrete data set accordingly.

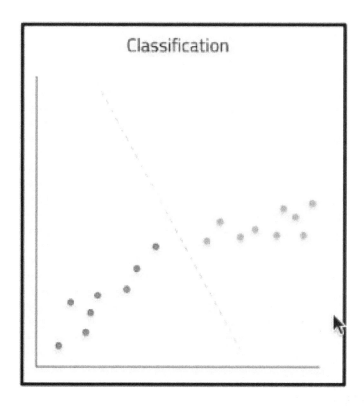

c. Clustering

This is a Machine Learning approach where the machine generates its own algorithms to differentiate among the data sets given in order to achieve the pre decided outcome. The data given is unlabelled and random. The machine computes the patterns out of the given data set of the training format and accordingly clusters the ones which follow the similar pattern. Here the output rules are different as per the patterns of recognition by the machine. For example, if you have a random data of stray cats which live in your locality, since you are unable to find any meaningful pattern amongst them, you would feed their data into the clustering algorithm. The algorithm would then analyse the data and divide them into clusters as per their similarities based on the noticed trends. The clusters are then given as output. Clustering hence works on discrete data sets.

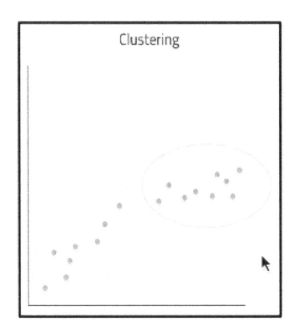

Note for Teachers

The aim is to familiarize students into understanding the AI Program. The foundation on which AI is built upon is Patterning; Data interpretation; Sorting; Comparing; Classifying; Identifying. The AI Applications that surround us are proof of innovation using technology. We need to prepare ourselves to unlearn, learn and relearn!

Evaluation

This stage follows the modelling and features various phases of testing. The stage of testing the models is figured as Evaluation. In this very process, the evaluation of each and every model is tried and the one which provides the most efficient and reliable output or the result is chosen. The evaluating process helps to Recognise different type of graphs and explore various patterns and trends out of the data explored.

Thus, to analyse the data, you need to visualise it in some user-friendly format so that you can:

- Quickly get a sense of the trends, relationships and patterns contained within the data.

- Define strategy for which model to use at a later stage.

- Communicate the same to others effectively. To visualise data, we can use various types of visual representations.

Deployment

This is by far a process to implement the surveillance system for the job or the project. This way the process implementation is able to catch hold the mischief of Mr. Robin and the mission gets accomplished!

The AI Project Cycle is now complete!

Applications of AI

The 10 ways AI, data science and technology are being used to manage and fight COVID-19 as a live project world over:

a. AI to identify, track and forecast outbreaks.

b. AI to help diagnose the virus.

c. Process health care claims.

d. Drones deliver medical supplies.

e. Robots sterilize, deliver food and supplies and perform other tasks.

f. Develop drugs.

g. Advanced fabrics offer protection.

h. AI to identify non-compliance or infected individuals.

i. Chatbots to share information

j. Supercomputers working on a coronavirus vaccine.

AI Applications and Integration as directed by the CBSE

a. AI Integration using GOOGLE Story Speaker. This is open for English learning. Viz.

Activity:

Write a newspaper article suggesting strategies to improve the food production in the country.

A discussion – "With the population rise in India more farmland areas is needed, while India is already intensively cultivated "Do you think Artificial Intelligence is the new way to solve this problem?"

_____

_____

_____

_____

_____

_____

_____

_____

_____

_____

_____

_____

_____

_____

_____

_____

b. AI Integration using Computer Vision. This is open as a live example for Science. Viz. Higher yields of food, say for example.

Activity:

What do you do to get higher yields in our farms?

Case Study – Why can we not make do with the current levels of agriculture production?

_____

_____

_____

_____

_____

_____

_____

_____

_____

_____

_____

_____

_____

_____

_____

_____

_____

_____

_____

c. AI Integration using Natural Language Processing (NLP) – Here we take Geography as a subject. Viz.

Activity:

Does climate impact gain production? How can you suggest ways to predict the climate and protect crop? What are the ideas you suggest for improving the natural irrigation system?

_____

_____

_____

_____

_____

_____

_____

_____

_____

_____

_____

_____

_____

_____

_____

_____

_____

d. AI Integration using Data Exploration – Here we take Mathematics as a subject of implementation for better learning.

Activity:

Problem Solving – Considering the population of India is more than one billion we need a quarter of a billion tonnes every year, what data will you collect to present your research report?

_____

_____

_____

_____

_____

_____

_____

_____

_____

_____

_____

_____

_____

_____

_____

_____

_____

_____

EXERCISES

Q1. Define the following terms:

    a. Problem Scoping

    b. Data Acquisition

    c. Data Exploration

    d. Modelling

Q2. What do you understand by Project Management of AI?

Q3. Name the various functions of AI Project Management.

Q4. What do you understand by the following:

    a. Learning

    b. Pattern Detection

    c. Data

    d. Self Programming

Q5. What are the various steps of AI Development Life Cycle?

Q6. Name the various skills required in the AI Field?

Q7. Name the various challenges acquired by AI?

Q8. Mention the steps of the AI Project Cycle with the help of a diagram.

Q9. Give an example of a Problem Scoping in AI.

Q10. What do you mean by Data Acquisition in AI. How do you acquire data using the 4Ws'.

Q11. What are the two types of data collected during the Acquisition process?

Q12. What do you mean by Data Exploration in AI. Give an example.

Q13. Write about the various data visualisation techniques available.

Q14. Define the term Data Modelling. Name the various Data Modelling formats.

Q15. Name the two types of Data Modelling.

Q16. Explain the Decision Tree Model of AI. With an example.

Q17. Explain the Pixel IT model of AI with an example.

Q18. Explain the following in brief:

    a. Regression

    b. Classification

    c. Clustering

Q19. What do you mean by Evaluation with reference to AI Project Cycle?

Q20. What do you mean by Deployment with reference to AI Project Cycle?

## CHAPTER 7

Neural Networks

What are Neural Networks?

As we well know about our brain, which is a combination of real biological neurons, similarly the Artificial Neural Network is a network or a circuit of neurons or nodes. This is used for solving artificial intelligence problems.

The human brain neuron is a cell within the nervous system which is the basic unit of the brain used to process and transmit information to all the other nerve cells and muscles. A network of such neurons is called a Neural Network.

In this chapter, we shall be studying about the Artificial Neural Network, which is a combinational model used in machine learning based on connected functions.

These systems "learn" to perform tasks by considering examples, generally without being programmed with task-specific rules.

Definition (As per CBSE – Resource)

Neural Networks are loosely modelled after how neurons in the human brain behave. The key advantage of neural networks are that they are able to extract data features automatically without needing the input of the programmer. A neural network is essentially a system of organizing machine learning algorithms to perform certain tasks. It is a fast and efficient way to solve problems for which the dataset is very large, such as in images.

Modelling of Neural Networks:

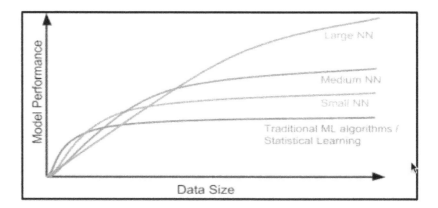

As per the above representation, the Neural Network tend to perform better with larger amount of data. This is quite unlike the traditional machine learning algorithms which stop the improvement after a specific saturation point in the process.

Importance of a Neural Network

The Neural Network have proved to be the most common and widely used algorithms which execute the deep learning and are used to solve the real life complex problems. This form of network can learn and create the relationships between all the inputs and complex problems and are able to extract data features automatically without any input by the programmer. One of the wide applications of this is the Facebook Image Tagging and automatic recommendation of Movies on Netflix.

Structure of a Neural Network

The Artificial Neural Network is a combination of neurons which are used to process the information. They consist of multiple layers and each layer is further divided into several blocks called nodes. Each node here has its own task to accomplish which is then passed to the next layers as follows:

a. Input Layer

b. Hidden Layer

c. Output Layer

The Input Layer is the first layer of the Neural Network. The work of this layer is to acquire data and feed it to the Neural Network. There is no processing during this layer.

The Hidden Layer is the layer where all the processing happens. This layer is hidden and is not visible to the users. Each node of these hidden layers has its own machine language algorithm which is executed as per the data given by the input layer. The executed output is then fed to the subsequent hidden layer of the network. As per the complexity of the function, there can be multiple hidden layers in a Neural Network System. Accordingly, the number of nodes in each layer can differ.

The Output Layer is the final output layer of the Neural Network System. The last hidden layer passes the final processed data to the output layer which further provides the final output. Hence, there is no processing in the Output Layer as the Input Layer in particular.

Important Features of Neural Network (Re-visited):

Neural Network Systems are modelled on the human brain and nervous system.

They are able to automatically extract features without input from the programmer.

Every Neural Node is essentially a machine learning algorithm.

It is useful when solving problems for which the data set is very large.

Neural Networks are trained in two formats:

a. Reinforcement Learning

b. Supervised Learning

Reinforcement Learning: (RL)

The reinforcement learning in terms of artificial intelligence is a type of dynamic programming that trains the algorithms using a system of reward and punishment. A reinforcement learning algorithm learns by interacting with its environment. This form of learning enables an agent to learn in an interactive environment by trial and error using feedback from its own actions and experiences. Here the algorithm is trained using data that is unlabelled.

Some of the key terms that describe the elements of a Reinforcement Learning problem are:

- Environment: This indicates the physical world in which agent operates.

- State: This explains the situation of the agent.

- Reward: This is the form of feedback from the environment.

- Policy: This is the way to map agent's state to actions.

- Value: This defines the future reward to be received by the agent after taking an action.

The Reinforcement Learning is a part of Machine Learning where an agent is put in an environment and he learns to behave in this environment by performing certain actions and observing the rewards which it gets from those actions. The reinforcement learning is mainly used in advanced machine learning areas such as self driving cars and so on.

Unsupervised Learning

The unsupervised learning is the training of the machine using information that is unlabelled and allowing the algorithm to act on that information without guidance.

The Unsupervised Learning is basically of two types:

a. Clustering

b. Association

The clustering is a method of dividing the objects into clusters which are similar between them and are dissimilar to the objects belonging to another cluster. For example which customer makes similar product purchases is clustering.

The Association is the about discovering the probability of the co-occurrence of times in a collection. For example, association would be which product was purchased by the customer.

For Example

A PacMan game can well be considered as a reinforcement learning problem. Here the goal of the agent (PacMan) is to eat the food in the grid while avoiding the ghosts on its way. The grid world is the interactive environment for the agent. PacMan receives a reward for eating food and punishment if it gets killed by the ghost (a loss occurs). The states are the location of PacMan in the grid world and the total cumulative reward is PacMan getting a win.

Hence the core of reinforcement learning is the concept that the optimal behaviour or action is reinforced by a positive reward. Depending on the complexity of the problem, reinforcement learning algorithms can keep adapting to the environment over time if necessary in order to maximise the reward in the long-term. It requires a lot of data which is why first applications for the technology have been in areas where simulated data is readily available such as in gameplay and robotics.

Supervised Learning (SL)

This type of learning in context of artificial intelligence and machine learning is a type of system in which both the input and the desired output data are provided. This works under supervision. Here the algorithm learns from a training dataset, which can be thought as the teacher. It uses classification algorithms and regression techniques to develop predictive models. It follows a feedback mechanism.

It is the machine learning task of learning a function that maps an input to an output based on example input-output pairs. Here each example is a pair consisting of an input object and a desired output value. Supervised Learning is basically of two types:

a. Classification – When the output variable is categorical i.e. with 2 or more classes (yes/no, true/false), we make use of classification.

b. Regression – Relationship between two or more variables where a change in one variable is associated with a change in other variable.

The supervised learning is used in the following:

a. Risk Assessment

b. Image Classification

c. Fraud Detection

d. Visual Recognition

For Example

If I say, "Will I get a salary raise or not?" this is Classification.

But if I say, "How much salary raise will I get?" this is Regression.

The algorithms include linear regression, logistic regression and neural networks as well, apart from decision tree, Support Vector Machine (SVM), random forest, naïve Bayes and K-nearest neighbour.

For Example

You may want to train a machine which helps you predict how long it will take you to drive home from your workplace.

	Supervised Learning	Unsupervised Learning	Reinforcement Learning
Definition	The machine learns by using labelled data.	The machine is trained on unlabelled data without and guidance.	An agent interacts with its environment by producing actions & discovers errors or rewards.
Type of Problems	Regression & Classification	Association & Clustering	Reward Based
Type of data	Labelled Data	Unlabelled Data	No pre-defined Data
Training	External Supervision	No Supervision	No Supervision
Approach	Map Labelled input to known output	Understand patterns and discover output	Follow trial and error method
Popular Algorithms	Linear Regression, Logistic Regression, Support Vector Machine, KNN etc.	K-Means, C-means, etc.	Q-Learning, SARSA, etc.

Supervised vs Unsupervised vs Reinforcement Learning

Regression	Classification	Clustering
• Supervised Learning	• Supervised Learning	• Unsupervised Learning
• Output as a continuous quantity	• Output is a categorical quantity	• Assigns data points into clusters
• Main aim is to forecast or predict	• Main aim is to compute the category of the data	• Main aim is to group similar items clusters
• Eg. Predict stock market price	• Eg. Classify emails as spam or non-spam	• Eg. Find all transactions which are fraudulent in nature
• Algorithm: Linear Regression	• Algorithm: Logistic Regression	• Algorithm: K-means

Regression vs Classification vs Clustering

Neural Networks Vs Nervous System

As per the brainfacts.org, Neurons are cells within the nervous system that transmit information to other nerve cells, muscle, or gland cells. Most neurons have a cell body, an axon, and dendrites.

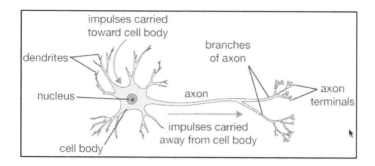

Picture Source: CBSE Resource

The cell body contains the nucleus and cytoplasm. The axon extends from the cell body and often gives rise to many smaller branches before ending at nerve terminals. Dendrites extend from the neuron cell body and receive message from other neurons. Synapses are the contact points where one neuron communicates with another. The dendrites are covered with synapses formed by the ends of axons from other neurons.

The Artificial Neural Network, on the other hand, the input layer gets data which is passed on to the nodes in the hidden layer.

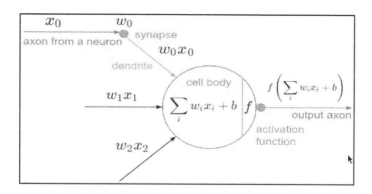

The nodes perform specific actions on the data and pass the processed information to the next layer. Finally the processed data is reached at the output stream through the output layer.

What is a Perceptron?

An Artificial Neuron or a Perceptron is a linear model used for binary classification. It models a neuron which has a set of inputs, each of which is given a specific weight. The neuron computes some function on these weighted inputs and gives the output.

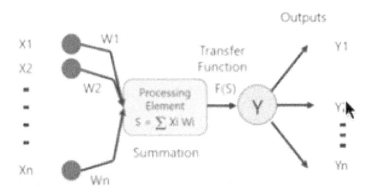

Artificial Neural Network

Perceptron or Artificial Neuron

ANN Vs BNN

ANN – Artificial Neural Network	BNN – Biological Neural Network	Function
Input Layer	Dendrites	Takes input for the system
Node	Cell Body	Responsible for processing of the information.
Interconnections	Synapse	These are the connections between the input and the output.
Output Layer	Axon	This sends out the result.

Activity

Students are recommended to perform live experiments on AI using the following link:

AI Experiments is a showcase for simple experiments that make it easier for anyone to start exploring machine learning, through pictures, drawings, language, music, and more.

Some of the interesting experiments are as follows:

a. What Neural Networks See

WHAT NEURAL NETWORKS SEE

by Gene Kogan

Explore the layers of a neural network with your camera.

b. Sketch RNN Demos

SKETCH-RNN DEMOS

by Ha / Jongejan / Johnson

Draw together with a neural network.

c. Autodraw

AUTODRAW

by Google Creative Lab

Fast drawing for everyone.

d. Quick, Draw!

QUICK, DRAW!

by Google Creative Lab

A game where a neural net tries to guess
what you're drawing.

Human Neural Network – The Game (As suggested by CBSE – Teachers' Resource)

Session Preparation:

Logistics: For a class of 40 students [Individual Activity]

Materials Required:

ITEM/Quantity

Images (To be kept with the facilitator)   2

Post-It Notes   80

Sketch-pens   40

Resources:

Purpose:

To understand and experience what neural network is like.

Brief:

Students will now experience how Neural Networks work with the help of an activity. Each of the students will be considered as the node of either Input Layer, 1st Hidden Layer, 2nd Hidden Layer or the Output Layer.

Ground Rules:

- No one is allowed to talk or discuss till the game ends. Fun of the game lies in playing it honestly.

- Each layer should sit distant to each other.

- The image should only be shown to the input layer and no one else.

- The game is supposed to be played silently. This means that one has to write a word on the chit and pass on the chit without speaking aloud.

- One needs to process the data as fast as possible, hence not take much time can be taken to write the pass on the chits.

- Input layer nodes cannot discuss the image shown with each other. Everyone has to use their own discretion.

- No sentences or multiple words are to be written on the chit. Only one word per chit is allowed.

- Once the task of a layer is finished, that layer needs to go and sit aside and not disturb others till the game ends.

Game Instructions:

Game Structure:

Layers	Number of Students	Number of chits
Input Layer	7	6
Hidden Layer 1	6	4
Hidden Layer 2	6	2
Output Layer	1	-
TOTAL	20	-

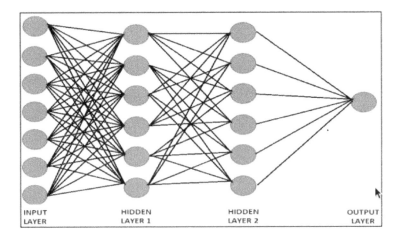

INPUT LAYER   HIDDEN LAYER 1   HIDDEN LAYER 2   OUTPUT LAYER

- Input Layer:

    a. 7 Students will be standing as the nodes of an input layer.

    b. All of them will be shown an image. After looking at it, they need to write 6 different words on 6 different chits. They have to choose the words which describe the image in the best way possible. They can also repeat the words if needed.

    c. After making these chits, they need to pass on one chit to each of the nodes of hidden layer 1. That is, 1 chit will be given to one member.

- Hidden Layer 1:

    a. 6 Students will be standing as the nodes of hidden layer 1.

    b. Each of them will receive 7 chits from 7 different input nodes. Now they have to take a good look at the chits and then write down 4 different words on 4 different chits. For this, they can either use the same words as the input layer did, or they can make their own information (relevant to the context) and write it.

    c. Now these 4 chits are to be given randomly to any 4 nodes of Hidden Layer 2. Out of the 6 nodes of 2nd hidden layer, one can choose any 4 and give once chit to each. (For best results, each node of hidden layer 2 should get almost same number of chits thus the division should be done properly)

- Hidden Layer 2:

    a. 6 students will be standing as the nodes of hidden layer 2.

    b. Each one of them will get some number of chits from the previous layer. Now they have to perform the same task as hidden layer 1 and have to write down 2 different words on 2 different chits and pass it on to the output layer.

- Output Layer:

    a. Finally the output layer node will get 12 chits. Now s/he has to understand all the words and has to guess which image was shown to the input layer initially.

    b. Output layer will then write a summary out of all the words received to explain his/her deduction. The summary should not be more than 5 lines.

- Finally, the output layer presents this summary in-front of everyone and the real image is finally revealed to all.

- If the summary is accurate enough, the whole network wins else they lose.

EXERCISE

Q1. What are Neural Networks in AI?

Q2. Write about the importance of Neural Networks in the real world.

Q3. Write about the structure of a Neural Network.

Q4. Name and explain the three layers of Artificial Neural Network.

Q5. Write about the important features of Neural Network.

Q6. Differentiate between Reinforcement Learning and Supervised Learning.

Q7. Name the elements of Reinforcement Learning.

Q8. Explain the following terms with reference to Unsupervised Learning:

   a. Clustering

   b. Association

Q9. Mention the fields where we use of the Supervised Learning.

Q10. Differentiate between Artificial Neural Networks and Nervous System (Biological Neural Network).

Q11. Make use of the following online applications at https://experiments.withgoogle.com/collection/ai and share your experience with your teacher.

Q12. Give the full form of the following:

   a. ANN

   b. BNN

   c. SL

   d. RL

## CHAPTER 8

Introduction to Python

Learning Objectives

Acquire introductory Python Programming Skills

Understand how AI projects can be run using Python

Introduction

A computer program is a set of instructions given to a computer to execute a particular task. There are many languages we use to write such programs for the computer. One of them is Python programming language. The other programming languages are BASIC, COBOL, C, C++, Java and others.

Python is a programming language which was developed by Guido Van Rossum when he was working at CWI (Centrum Wiskunde & Informatica) which is a National Research Institute for Mathematics and Computer Science in Netherlands. The language was released in 1991. Python got its name from a BBC comedy series from seventies – "Monty Python's Flying Circus."

It terms of Guido van Rossum, "Python is an experiment in how much freedom program-mers need. Too much freedom and nobody can read another's code; too little and expressive-ness is endangered."

StackOverflow calls python as the fastest growing programming language. Python is an open-source, object-oriented programming language mainly used for Data Science.

Why was python created?

As per the developer, Guido Van Rossum,

"My original motivation for creating Python was the perceived need for a higher level language in the Amoeba [Operating Systems] project. I realised that the development of system administration utilities in C was taking too long. Moreover, doing these things in the Bourne shell wouldn't work for a variety of reasons. ...... So, there was a need for a language that would bridge the gap between C and the shell."

Features of Python

- Python is a general purpose programming language that is often applied in scripting roles.
- It is object-oriented.
- Indentation is one of the greatest features in Python.
- It is free (open source), which means downloading and installing Python is free and easy. The source code is easily accessible.
- It is mixable, can be linked to components written in other languages easily. The linking is fast and integrated.
- It is easy to use and easy to learn.
- It is a platform independent programming language.

Use of Python

Python is commonly used by programmers to:

- Program video games
- Build Artificial Intelligence Algorithms
- Program various scientific programs such as statistical models.

Installing Python

To write and run Python program, we need to have Python Interpreter installed in our computer. IDLE (GUI integrated) is the standard and the most popular Python development environment. IDLE is an acronym of Integrated Development Environment. It allows edit, run, browse and debug Python Programs from a single interface. This environment allows easy coding of programs.

For windows Operating Systems, user can download from https://www.python.org/downloads/

The link has the latest version of python IDE (Integrated Development Environment).

We get the oscreen as follows:

We will be using Python 3.8.2 of Python IDLE to develop and run Python code in this book. It can be downloaded from **www.python. org/downloads/**

After installing the Python, go to start menu then click on Python 3.8.2 and click on Python IDLE to get the above command line screen.

We get a welcome message of Python interpreter with version details and the Python prompt **>>>**

>>> is the Primary prompt and indicates that the interpreter is ready for the instructions.

Modes of Working in Python IDLE

We can work in two ways:

a. Interactive Mode

b. Script Mode

- The Interactive Mode allows us to interact with OS;

- The Script Mode lets us execute and edit the python source files.

Sample working on Interactive Mode:

```
●  ◎  ●                        Python 3.8.2 Shell
Python 3.8.2 (v3.8.2:7b3ab5921f, Feb 24 2020, 17:52:18)
[Clang 6.0 (clang-600.0.57)] on darwin
Type "help", "copyright", "credits" or "license()" for more information.
>>> print("Hello, this is Sumit")
Hello, this is Sumit
>>> print("Today is a holiday")
Today is a holiday
>>> print(10+30)
40
>>> |




                                                      Ln: 10   Col: 4
```

We type the python expression/statement/command after the prompt and Python immediately responds with the output.

>>> print("Hello, this is Sumit")

Hello, this is Sumit

>>> print("Today is a holiday")

Today is a holiday

>>> print(10+30)

40

>>>

Using the Script Mode:

This mode allows the creation of a script or a file name with an extension of .py

By convention all Python program files have names which end with .py

We follow the following steps:

File>New File

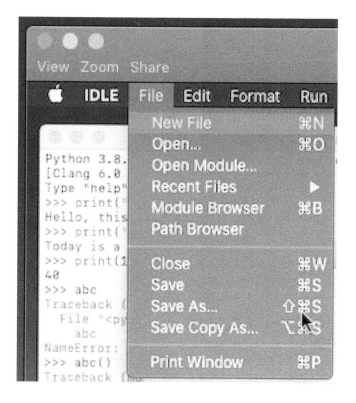

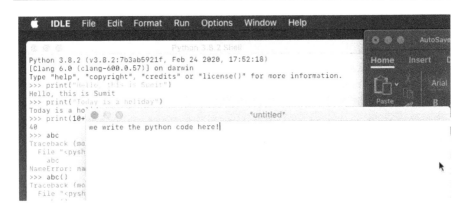

Coding the Program:

We write a simple program here to assign two numbers, and print the sum using the third variable z.

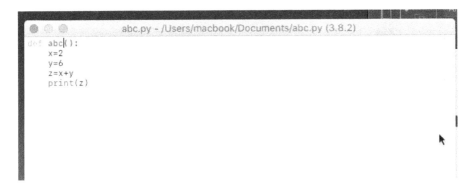

The code is saved using the save option as abc.py

To Execute the above program, we select RUN.

Or we can execute the file using the file name followed by parenthesis as:

abc()

```
Python 3.8.2 Shell
Python 3.8.2 (v3.8.2:7b3ab5921f, Feb 24 2020, 17:52:18)
[Clang 6.0 (clang-600.0.57)] on darwin
Type "help", "copyright", "credits" or "license()" for more information.
>>>
=================== RESTART: /Users/macbook/Documents/abc.py ===================
>>> abc()
8
>>> |
                                                              Ln: 8   Col: 4
```

Fundamentals of Python Programming

We shall study the following in order to understand the basics of Python Programming:

a. Python Variables

b. Python Data Types

c. Python Operators

d. Python Statements

e. Python Functions

Variables and Types

Likewise any programming language, variables in Python are memory spaces where values get stored. It is the object's address in memory and does not change once it has been created.

The variables need no declaration in Python. They are referred as objects. The value that you have stored may change in the future according to the specifications.

Variable Definition & Declaration

Python has no additional commands to declare a variable. As soon as the value is assigned to it, the variable is declared.

Eg. x=20

Variable x is declared as the value 20 is assigned.

The following are the data types of Variables:

a. Number – It represents the numeric values and further supports 4 sub types as well. Following are the sub-types of numerical data type:

   i. Integers – They represent whole number values.

   ii. Float – The represent decimal point values.

   iii. Complex Numbers – The represent imaginary values and are denoted with 'j' at the end of the number.

   iv. Boolean: It is used to represent the categorical output, since the output of Boolean is either true or false.

We can convert the integer value to a float value or vice versa in Python language using the following order:

A=90

B=float(A)

Print(B)

The above code shall convert an integer A to float type B.

a. Strings – The strings in python represent the Unicode character values. A single character is also considered as a string. Eg. Name = 'amit'

b. Lists – The List is one of the four collection data type that we have in Python. This is similar to arrays in any other programming language. It is an ordered and changeable format, unlike the strings. We can add duplicate values as well.

To declare a list we use the square brackets.

Eg. mylist = [10,20,30,40,20,30, 'INDIA']

   print(mylist)

c. Tuples – It is a collection which is unchangeable or immutable. It is ordered and the values can be accessed using the index values. A tuple can have duplicate values as well. To declare a tuple we use the round brackets.

Eg. mytuple = (10,10,20,30,40,50)

   Since a tuple is unchangeable once you have declared it, there are not many operations you can perform on a tuple. But there is a bright side to using a tuple, you can store values in a tuple which you do not want to change wile working in a project.

d. Sets – A set is a collection which is unordered, it does not have any indexes. To declare a set in python we use the curly brackets.

Eg. myset = {12, 23, 22, 44, 33}

   A set done not have any duplicate values, even though it will not show any errors while declaring the set, the output only displays the distinct values in particular. Python's set class represents the mathematical notion of a set. The major advantage of using a set, as opposed to a list, is that it has a highly optimized method for checking whether a specific element is contained in the set. This is based on a data structure known as a hash table.

Some of the set operations are:

Union – Two sets can be merged using union() function or | operator.

Eg. Example:

A = {10,20,30}

B={50,30,12}

Print(A|B)

Output:

{50, 20, 10, 12, 30}

Intersection – The Intersection() or & operator and is used to find the common elements of the two sets.

Example:

A = {10,20,30}

B={50,30,12}

print(A & B)

output:

{30}

Difference – To find the difference in between sets. This is done through difference() or – operator.

Example:

A = {10,20,30}

B={50,30,12}

print(A-B)

Output:

{10, 20}

Symmetric Difference – This returns the elements of both the sets except the common elements. It is performed using the ^ operator.

Example:

```
A = {10,20,30}
B={50,30,12}
print(A^B)
```

Output:

```
{10, 12, 50, 20}
```

a. Dictionary – A dictionary is just like any other collection array in Python. It is unordered and changeable.

Eg.

```
mydictionary = {'Name': 'Abhishek', 'Class': 'IX-B'}
print(mydictionary)
```

Output:

```
{'Name': 'Abhishek', 'Class': 'IX-B'}
```

If we give:

```
>>> print(mydictionary['Name'])
```

Output:

```
Abhishek
```

We can change the elements in a dictionary as:

```
mydictionary['Class']='IX-C'
print(mydictionary['Class'])
```

Output:

```
>>> print(mydictionary['Class'])
IX-C
```

Operators in Python

Like any programming language, Python also has a set of operators used for computational and logical operations within the program.

It supports the following types of operators:

Arithmetic Operators

The arithmetic operators are used with numeric values to perform common mathematical operations as follows:

Operator	Name	Example
+	Addition	x+y
-	Subtraction	x-y
*	Multiplication	x*y
/	Division	x/y
%	Modulus	x%y
**	Exponentiation	x**y
//	Floor division	x//y

Example of Usage:

```
x = 10
y = 2
print(x + y)
print(x-y)
print(x*y)
print(x/y)
print(x%y)
print(x//y)
```

Sample Output:

12

8

20

5.0

0

5

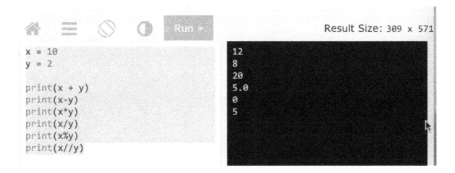

Assignment Operators

These operators are used to assign values to variables and are of following types:

Operator	Example	Meaning
=	a=5	a=5
+=	a+=3	a=a+3
-=	a-=3	a=a-3
*=	a*=4	a=a*4
/=	a/=4	a=a/4
%=	a%=2	a=a%2
//=	a//=3	a=a//3

**=	a**=3	a=a**3
&=	a&=3	a=a&3
|=	a|=3	a=a|3
^=	a^=3	a=a^3
>>=	a>>=3	a=a>>3
<<=	a<<=3	a=a<<3

Example:

```
a=5
a=a*4
print(a)
a=5
a=a/4
print(a)
a=5
a=a%2
print(a)
a=5
a=a//3
print(a)
a=5
a=a**3
print(a)
a=5
a=a&3
print(a)
```

```
a=5
a=a|3
print(a)
a=5
a=a^3
print(a)
a=5
a=a>>3
print(a)
a=5
a=a<<3
print(a)
```

Output:

```
8
2
20
1.25
1
1
125
1
7
6
0
40
```

Comparison Operators

The comparison operators in Python are used to compare two values are are as follows:

Operator	Name	Example
==	Equal	a == b
!=	Not Equal	a != b
>	Greater than	a > b
<	Less than	a < b
>=	Greater than or equal to	a >= b
<=	Less than or equal to	a <= b

Example:

```
a = 50
b = 30
print(a == b)
print(a != b)
print(a > b)
print(a < b)
print(a>=b)
print(a<=b)
```

Output:

```
False
True
True
False
True
False
```

Logical Operators

The logical operators provide combination of conditional statements in Python programming.

The following are the logical operators in use:

Operator	Function	Example
and	Returns True if both statements are true	a < 10 and a < 20
or	Returns True if one of the statements is true	a < 10 or a<20
not	Reverses the result, returns False if the result is true	not(a<10 and a<20)

Example:

```
a = 15
print(a<10 and a<20)
print(a<10 or a<20)
print(not(a<10 and a<20))
```

Output:

```
False
True
True
```

Identity Operators

The Identity Operators in Python are used to compare the objects. They check if the two variables are located on the same part of the memory. The two variables or objects which are equal may not mean that they are identical in nature.

The Identity Operators are as follows:

Operator	Description	Example
is	Returns True if both the variables are the same object.	a is b
is not	Returns True if both variables are not the same object.	a is not y

Example:

```
a = ["orange", "apple"]
b = ["orange", "apple"]
c = b
print(c is b)
print(a is b)
print(a == b)
print(a is not b)
```

Output:

```
True
False
True
True
```

Membership Operators

The membership operators are used to test if a sequence is presented in an object. In a way it is used to test whether a variable is found in a sequence or not.

They are of following types:

Operator	Description	Example
In	Returns True if a Sequence with the specified Value is present in the object.	a in b
not in	Returns True if a sequence with the specified value is not present in the object	a not in b

Example:

a = ["cricket", "football"]

print("football" in a)

print("vollyball" in a)

Output:

True

False

Conditional Statements of Python

Python offers the use of conditional statements to execute a statement or a group of statements with the checking of conditions.

There are three conditional statements of Python, viz.

If

Elif

Else

An 'if statement' is written by using the if keyword.

Example:

```
a = 20
b = 30
if b>a:
    print("b is greater than a")
```

In the above example:

The two variables are a and b. If the condition b>a is **true** we get the execution of the statement "print("b is greater than a").

Elif is another conditional statement of Python. The elif keyword is a way to direct the machine to try the next condition if the previous 'if' is false.

Eg.

```
a = 20
b = 20
if b>a:
    print("b is greater than a")
elif a==b:
    print("a and b are both equal")
```

Here on execution of the program:

The control fetches to the elif section and hence the execution of

"print("a and b are both equal")" is done.

We get the output as:

a and b are both equal

Else

The else keyword catches and executes anything which is not encountered by the earlier if or elif.

Example:

```
a = 300
b = 30
if b>a:
    print("b is greater than a")
elif a==b:
    print("a and b are both equal")
else:
    print("a is greater than b")
```

Here we get the output as:

a is greater than b

Looping in Python

The looping in Python indicates the execution of a set of instructions multiple times. The following are the various looping statements in Python.

While Loop

In python, while loop is used to execute a block of statements repeatedly until a given condition is satisfied. And when the condition becomes false, the statements after the loop is executed. It repeats the execution as long as a certain Boolean condition is met.

For Example:

```
counter =0
while counter<5:
    print(counter)
    counter +=1
```

Output:

    0

    1

    2

    3

    4

For Loop

The for loop can iterate over a sequence of numbers using the "range" functions. It allows a part of the code to be repeated a limited number of times.

For Example:

```
for x in range(5):
    print(x)
```

Output:

    0

    1

    2

    3

    4

Another example:

```
fruits=["banana", "apple", "orange"]
For a in fruits:
    print(x)
```

Output:

banana

apple

orange

Nested Loop

Loops can also be nested in Python as in other programming languages. It is also known as a loop within a loop.

For Example:

```
for i in range(1,6):
for j in range(i):
print("*", end=' ')
print()
```

Output:

```
*
* *
* * *
* * * *
* * * * *
```

Loop Control Statements in Python

In order to break out of any normal execution in a loop, we make use of loop control statements in Python as follows:

break, continue and pass as:

Use of break

The break statement stops the execution and shifts the control to the next statement outside its block.

Example:

```
for i in "home":
    print(i)
    if i=='m':break;
```

Output:

```
h

o

m
```

Use of continue

The continue statement skips the statement after continue and shifts the control to the next item in the sequence.

For Example:

```
for i in "home":
    if i=='m': continue
    print(i)
```

Output:

```
h

o

e
```

Use of pass

The pass statement is a null statement. The interpreter does not ignore it, but it performs a no-operation.

Example:

```
for i in "home":
    if i=='m': pass
    print(i)
```

Output:

```
h

o

m

e
```

Functions in Python

Functions in Python are the blocks of code which only runs when it is called. The data is passed as parameters into a function. The functions can return data as a specific result.

We have already used some of the built-in functions like print(), but we can create our own functions and we term them as user-defined functions.

A function in Python is defined using the following simple steps:

- A function block always begins with the keyword def and is followed by the function name and parentheses.

- The input parameters are placed within the parentheses.

- The first statement of a function can be an optional statement.

- The code block within every functions starts with a colon and is indented.

- A return statement exits a function which may not have a return type.

Creating a Function in Python

We create a function using the def keyword as follows:

```
def my_function():
    Print('Hi, How are you doing today?')
```

Calling a Function

In order to call a function, we use the name of the function name followed by the parenthesis as follows:

```
my_function()
```

Output:

Hi, How are you doing today?

Arguments within Functions

We can pass information into functions as arguments as follows:

```
def my_function(myname):
    print(myname+" Hafeez")
my_function("Ismail")
my_function("Roza")
my_function("Arvind")
```

Output:

Ismail Hafeez

Roza Hafeez

Arvind Hafeez

Please note that by default, a function must be called with the correct number of arguments. If your function expects two arguments, you have to call the function with two arguments.

Input in Python

We make use of input() function to ask a user for some text input. We may call this function to tell the program to even stop and wait for the user to key in the data. The Python 3 as a input() function to execute this task. It has the following format:

The input() function allows an input in the specified variable.

Example:

```
print("Enter your name:")

x = input()

print("Hello, " + x)
```

Output:

```
Enter your name:
Dheeraj
Hello, Dheeraj
```

Remark/Comment in Python

We make use of # sign for giving a remark or a comment in Python.

```
# This is comment in Python
```

Example Programs in Python

Program #1:

Program to add the given two numbers:

```
# Program to add two numbers
num1 = 100
num2 = 120
# Adding two nos
sum = num1 + num2
# printing values
print("Sum of two number is", sum)
```

Sample Output:

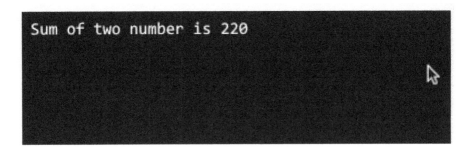

```
Sum of two number is 220
```

Program #2:

To input any two numbers and display the sum.

```
# Program to add two numbers
number1 = input("First number: ")
number2 = input("\nSecond number: ")
# Adding two numbers
# User might also enter float numbers
sumofnumbers = float(number1) + float(number2)
```

Display the sum

print("The sum of numbers is", sumofnumbers)

```
# abc.py - /Users/macbook/Documents/abc.py (3.8.2)
# Program to add two numbers

number1 = input("First number: ")
number2 = input("\nSecond number: ")

# Adding two numbers
# User might also enter float numbers

sumofnumbers =  float(number1) + float(number2)

# Display the sum


print("The sum of numbers is ",sumofnumbers)
```

Output:

```
# Python 3.8.2 Shell
Python 3.8.2 (v3.8.2:7b3ab5921f, Feb 24 2020, 17:52:18)
[Clang 6.0 (clang-600.0.57)] on darwin
Type "help", "copyright", "credits" or "license()" for more information.
>>>
=================== RESTART: /Users/macbook/Documents/abc.py ===================
First number: 12

Second number: 24
The sum of numbers is  36.0
>>>
```

Program #3:

Program to print the Fibonacci series.

The Fibonacci numbers are the numbers in the following integer sequence.

0, 1, 1, 2, 3, 5, 8, 13, 21, 34, 55, 89, 144, ...

Solution:

Function for printing the first 10 terms of the fibonacci series

Taking 1st two fibonacci numbers as 0 and 1

```python
def fibonacci(n):
a = 0
b = 1
print(a)
print(b)
# First two elements are already printed here.
if n < 0:
print("Incorrect input")
elif n == 0:
return a
elif n == 1:
return b
else:
for i in range(2,n):
c = a + b
print(c)
a = b
b = c
# Call of the function
print(fibonacci(10))
```

```
●  ●  ●              *abc.py - /Users/macbook/Documents/abc.py (3.8.2)*

# Function for printing the first 10 terms of the fibonacci series
# Taking 1st two fibonacci numbers as 0 and 1

def fibonacci(n):
    a = 0
    b = 1
    print(a)
    print(b)
  # First two elements are already printed here.
    if n < 0:
        print("Incorrect input")
    elif n == 0:
        return a
    elif n == 1:
        return b
    else:
        for i in range(2,n):
            c = a + b
            print(c)
            a = b
            b = c

| # Call of the function
print(fibonacci(10))

                                                    Ln: 24    Col: 0
```

Solution:

```
●  ●  ●                  Python 3.8.2 Shell
Python 3.8.2 (v3.8.2:7b3ab5921f, Feb 24 2020, 17:52:18)
[Clang 6.0 (clang-600.0.57)] on darwin
Type "help", "copyright", "credits" or "license()" for more inform
ation.
>>>
==================== RESTART: /Users/macbook/Documents/abc.py =====
==============
0
1
1
2
3
5
8
13
21
34
None
>>> |

                                                    Ln: 17    Col: 4
```

Program #4

Program to print the following pattern:

```
1
1 1
1 1 1
1 1 1 1
1 1 1 1 1
```

```python
# printing pattern
print("The pattern required is as follows")
for row in range(0,5):
for column in range(0,row+1):
print("1", end="")
# ending line
print('\r')
# To get the control to the next line once the loop is over.
```

Output:

```
                         Python 3.8.2 Shell
Python 3.8.2 (v3.8.2:7b3ab5921f, Feb 24 2020, 17:52:18)
[Clang 6.0 (clang-600.0.57)] on darwin
Type "help", "copyright", "credits" or "license()" for more information.
>>>
=================== RESTART: /Users/macbook/Documents/abc.py ===================
The pattern required is as follows
1

1 1

1 1 1

1 1 1 1

1 1 1 1 1
>>> |
                                                        Ln: 12   Col: 4
```

Program #5

Program to display the following format:

1

12

123

1234

Program:

```
# printing pattern
print("The pattern required is as follows")
for row in range(0,5):
for column in range(1,row+1):
print(column,end="")
# ending line
print('\r')
# To get the control to the next line once the loop is over.
```

```
abc.py - /Users/macbook/Documents/abc.py (3.8.2)
# printing pattern
print("The pattern required is as follows")
for row in range(0,5):


    for column in range(1,row+1):
        print(column,end="")

    # ending line
    print('\r')
    # To get the control to the next line once the loop is over.
```

Ln: 16   Col: 0

Output:

```
Python 3.8.2 Shell
Python 3.8.2 (v3.8.2:7b3ab5921f, Feb 24 2020, 17:52:18)
[Clang 6.0 (clang-600.0.57)] on darwin
Type "help", "copyright", "credits" or "license()" for more information.
>>>
================== RESTART: /Users/macbook/Documents/abc.py ==================
The pattern required is as follows

1

12

123

1234

>>> |
                                                              Ln: 12   Col: 4
```

Program #6

Program to print the following pattern:

```
*

* *

* * *

* * * *
```

Code:

```python
# printing pattern
print("The pattern required is as follows")
for row in range(0,5):
for column in range(1,row+1):
print('*',end="")
# ending line
print('\r')
# To get the control to the next line once the loop is over.
```

```
abc.py - /Users/macbook/Documents/abc.py (3.8.2)
# printing pattern

print("The pattern required is as follows")

for row in range(0,5):



    for column in range(1,row+1):
        print('*',end="")

    # ending line
    print('\r')
    # To get the control to the next line once the loop is over.

|
```

Ln: 16   Col: 0

Output:

```
Python 3.8.2 Shell
Python 3.8.2 (v3.8.2:7b3ab5921f, Feb 24 2020, 17:52:18)
[Clang 6.0 (clang-600.0.57)] on darwin
Type "help", "copyright", "credits" or "license()" for more information.
>>>
==================== RESTART: /Users/macbook/Documents/abc.py ====================
The pattern required is as follows

*

**

***

****

>>> |
```

Ln: 12   Col: 4

Program #7

Program to display the following pattern:

```
1
1 2
1 2 3
1 2 3 4
1 2 3 4 5
1 2 3 4 5 6
1 2 3 4 5 6 7
1 2 3 4 5 6 7 8
1 2 3 4 5 6 7 8 9
1 2 3 4 5 6 7 8 9 10
```

Code:

```
#Printing of a pattern
for r in range (0, 10):
a = 1
for column in range (0, r+1):
print(a, end=" ")
a = a+1
# ending line
print('\r')
```

```
● ◎ ●   *abc.py - /Users/macbook/Documents/abc.py (3.8.2)*
#Printing of a pattern
for r in range (0, 10):
    a = 1

    for column in range (0, r+1):
        print(a, end=" ")
        a = a+1
    # ending line
    print('\r')
|
                                                    Ln: 10   Col: 0
```

Output:

```
● ● ●                        Python 3.8.2 Shell
Python 3.8.2 (v3.8.2:7b3ab5921f, Feb 24 2020, 17:52:18)
[Clang 6.0 (clang-600.0.57)] on darwin
Type "help", "copyright", "credits" or "license()" for more information.
>>>
=================== RESTART: /Users/macbook/Documents/abc.py ===================
1

1 2

1 2 3

1 2 3 4

1 2 3 4 5

1 2 3 4 5 6

1 2 3 4 5 6 7

1 2 3 4 5 6 7 8

1 2 3 4 5 6 7 8 9

1 2 3 4 5 6 7 8 9 10

>>> |
                                                    Ln: 16   Col: 4
```

Program #8

Program to print the following pattern:

    1

    2 3

    4 5 6

    7 8 9 10

    11 12 13 14 15

    16 17 18 19 20 21

Code:

```
#Printing of a pattern as required
n = 1
#row operation
for r in range (0, 6):
# column operation
for column in range (0, r+1):
print(n, end=" ")
n = n+1
# ending line
print('\r')
```

```
●  ◉  ◉      abc.py - /Users/macbook/Documents/abc.py (3.8.2)
#Printing of a pattern as required
n = 1
#row operation
for r in range (0, 6):

    # column operation
    for column in range (0, r+1):
        print(n, end=" ")
        n = n+1
    # ending line
    print('\r')
|
```

                                                    Ln: 12   Col: 0

Output:

```
◉  ◉  ◉                    Python 3.8.2 Shell
Python 3.8.2 (v3.8.2:7b3ab5921f, Feb 24 2020, 17:52:18)
[Clang 6.0 (clang-600.0.57)] on darwin
Type "help", "copyright", "credits" or "license()" for more information.
>>>
==================== RESTART: /Users/macbook/Documents/abc.py ====================
1

2 3

4 5 6

7 8 9 10

11 12 13 14 15

16 17 18 19 20 21

>>>
```

                                                    Ln: 12   Col: 4

Program #9

Program to Calculate the Average of Numbers in an entered list of numbers.

n=int(input("Enter the number of elements to be averaged "))

a=[]

for i in range(0,n):

elem=int(input("Enter the number please: "))

a.append(elem)

avg=sum(a)/n

print("The Average of numbers in the list is:", round(avg,2))

```
n=int(input("Enter the number of elements to be averaged "))
a=[]
for i in range(0,n):
    elem=int(input("Enter the number please: "))
    a.append(elem)
avg=sum(a)/n
print("The Average of numbers in the list is: ",round(avg,2))
```

                                                      Ln: 8   Col: 0

Output:

```
Python 3.8.2 Shell
Python 3.8.2 (v3.8.2:7b3ab5921f, Feb 24 2020, 17:52:18)
[Clang 6.0 (clang-600.0.57)] on darwin
Type "help", "copyright", "credits" or "license()" for more information.
>>>
==================== RESTART: /Users/macbook/Documents/abc.py ====================
Enter the number of elements to be averaged 4
Enter the number please: 12
Enter the number please: 13
Enter the number please: 14
Enter the number please: 15
The Average of numbers in the list is:  13.5
>>>
```

                                                      Ln: 12   Col: 4

Program #10

Program to input any number and print its reverse.

Input: 123

Output: 321

Code:

```
# Program to print the reverse of any entered number
n=int(input("Please Enter any number: "))
rev=0
number=n
while(n>0):
digit=n%10
rev=rev*10+digit
n=n//10
print("Reverse of the number:",number)
print("is",rev)
```

```
abc.py - /Users/macbook/Documents/abc.py (3.8.2)
# Program to print the reverse of any entered number
n=int(input("Please Enter any number: "))
rev=0
number=n
while(n>0):
    digit=n%10
    rev=rev*10+digit
    n=n//10
print("Reverse of the number:",number)
print("is",rev)

                                          Ln: 12   Col: 0
```

Output:

```
                                      Python 3.8.2 Shell
Python 3.8.2 (v3.8.2:7b3ab5921f, Feb 24 2020, 17:52:18)
[Clang 6.0 (clang-600.0.57)] on darwin
Type "help", "copyright", "credits" or "license()" for more information.
>>>
=================== RESTART: /Users/macbook/Documents/abc.py ===================
Please Enter any number: 123
Reverse of the number: 123
is 321
>>>

                                                                    Ln: 9   Col: 4
```

Program #11

Program to enter a number and print the sum of the digits.

Input: 123

Output: 6

Program to print the sum of digits of any entered number

n=int(input("Please Enter any number: "))

sumnum=0

number=n

while(n>0):

digit=n%10

sumnum=sumnum+digit

n=n//10

print("Sum of digits of the number is:",sumnum)

```
abc.py - /Users/macbook/Documents/abc.py (3.8.2)
# Program to print the sum of digits of any entered number
n=int(input("Please Enter any number: "))
sumnum=0
number=n
while(n>0):
    digit=n%10
    sumnum=sumnum+digit
    n=n//10
print("Sum of digits of the number is:",sumnum)

I
                                                     Ln: 12   Col: 0
```

Output:

```
                        Python 3.8.2 Shell
Python 3.8.2 (v3.8.2:7b3ab5921f, Feb 24 2020, 17:52:18)
[Clang 6.0 (clang-600.0.57)] on darwin
Type "help", "copyright", "credits" or "license()" for more information.
>>>
=================== RESTART: /Users/macbook/Documents/abc.py ===================
Please Enter any number: 123
Sum of digits of the number is: 6
>>>


                                                     Ln: 8   Col: 4
```

Program #12

Program to input a number and count its number of digits.

Input: 234

Output: 3

Program to print the number of digits of any entered number

n=int(input("Please Enter any number: "))

countnum=0

number=n

while(n>0):

digit=n%10

countnum=countnum+1

n=n//10

print("The number of digits of the number is:",countnum)

```
● ◎ ●        abc.py - /Users/macbook/Documents/abc.py (3.8.2)
# Program to print the number of digits of any entered number
n=int(input("Please Enter any number: "))
countnum=0
number=n
while(n>0):
    digit=n%10
    countnum=countnum+1|
    n=n//10
print("The number of digits of the number is:",countnum)
```
Ln: 7   Col: 23

Output:

```
● ◎ ●                    Python 3.8.2 Shell
Python 3.8.2 (v3.8.2:7b3ab5921f, Feb 24 2020, 17:52:18)
[Clang 6.0 (clang-600.0.57)] on darwin
Type "help", "copyright", "credits" or "license()" for more information.
>>>
=================== RESTART: /Users/macbook/Documents/abc.py ==================
Please Enter any number: 5433
The number of digits of the number is: 4
>>> |
```
Ln: 8   Col: 4

Program #13

Program to enter a number and check if it is a palindrome. A number is said to be a palindrome if it is equal to its reverse.

Input: 121

It is a palindrome.

Input: 123

It is not a palindrome.

```python
# Program
n=int(input("Please Enter any number: "))
rev=0
number=n
while(n>0):
digit=n%10
rev=rev*10+digit
n=n//10
print("Reverse of the number:",number)
print("is",rev)
if (number==rev):
print("Palindrome")
else:
print("The number is not a palindrome")
```

```python
# Program to input a number and check if it is a palindrome.
n=int(input("Please Enter any number: "))
rev=0
number=n
while(n>0):
    digit=n%10
    rev=rev*10+digit
    n=n//10
print("Reverse of the number:",number)
print("is",rev)
if (number==rev):

    print("Palindrome")
else:
    print("The number is not a palindrome")
```

Ln: 1   Col: 60

Output:

```
●  ●  ●                    Python 3.8.2 Shell
Python 3.8.2 (v3.8.2:7b3ab5921f, Feb 24 2020, 17:52:18)
[Clang 6.0 (clang-600.0.57)] on darwin
Type "help", "copyright", "credits" or "license()" for more information.
>>>
=================== RESTART: /Users/macbook/Documents/abc.py ===================
Please Enter any number: 1221
Reverse of the number: 1221
is 1221
Palindrome
>>> |
                                                          Ln: 10   Col: 4
```

Program #14

Program to print the table of a given number:

Solution:

n=int(input("Enter the number to print the tables for:"))

print("The table of the entered number",n," is as follows")

for i in range(1,11):

print(n,"x",i,"=",n*i)

print("Program over")

```
●  ●  ●    abc.py - /Users/macbook/Documents/abc.py (3.8.2)
n=int(input("Enter the number to print the tables for:"))
print("The table of the entered number",n," is as follows")
for i in range(1,11):
    print(n,"x",i,"=",n*i)
print("Program over")
|



                                                          Ln: 6   Col: 0
```

Solution:

```
Python 3.8.2 Shell
Python 3.8.2 (v3.8.2:7b3ab5921f, Feb 24 2020, 17:52:18)
[Clang 6.0 (clang-600.0.57)] on darwin
Type "help", "copyright", "credits" or "license()" for more information.
>>>
==================== RESTART: /Users/macbook/Documents/abc.py ====================
Enter the number to print the tables for:12
The table of the entered number 12  is as follows
12 x 1 = 12
12 x 2 = 24
12 x 3 = 36
12 x 4 = 48
12 x 5 = 60
12 x 6 = 72
12 x 7 = 84
12 x 8 = 96
12 x 9 = 108
12 x 10 = 120
Program over
>>>
                                                                    Ln: 19   Col: 4
```

Program #15

Program to input a number and check if it is an Armstrong Number or not. An Armstrong Number is a number whose sum of the cube of digits is equal to the original number.

Solution:

Python program to check if the number is an Armstrong number or not

take input from the user

num = int(input("Enter a number: "))

Program to enter a number and check if it is an amstrong number

initialize sum as zero value

sum = 0

Calculating the sum of the cube of each digit

temp = num

while temp > 0:

```
digit = temp % 10

sum += digit ** 3

temp //= 10

# printing the result

if num == sum:

print(num,"is an Armstrong number")

else:

print(num,"is not an Armstrong number")

print("The Program is Over now!")
```

```
# Python program to check if the number is an Armstrong number or

# take input from the user
num = int(input("Enter a number: "))
# Program to enter a number and check if it is an amstrong number
# initialize sum as zero value
sum = 0

# Calculating the sum of the cube of each digit
temp = num
while temp > 0:
    digit = temp % 10
    sum += digit ** 3
    temp //= 10|

# printing the result
if num == sum:
    print(num,"is an Armstrong number")
else:
    print(num,"is not an Armstrong number")
    print("The Program is Over now!")
```

Ln: 14   Col: 14

Output:

```
                              Python 3.8.2 Shell
Python 3.8.2 (v3.8.2:7b3ab5921f, Feb 24 2020, 17:52:18)
[Clang 6.0 (clang-600.0.57)] on darwin
Type "help", "copyright", "credits" or "license()" for more information.
>>>
==================== RESTART: /Users/macbook/Documents/abc.py ====================
Enter a number: 153
153 is an Armstrong number
>>> |
                                                          Ln: 8   Col: 4
```

Program #16

Program to find the sum of elements stored in a List.

```python
# Python program to find sum of elements in list
total = 0
# creating a list
list1 = [10, 20, 30, 40, 50]
# Taking a list and computing each element in Total
for ele in range(0, len(list1)):
    total = total + list1[ele]
# printing total value
print("Sum of all elements in given list: ", total)
print("program over")
```

```
● ● ●        abc.py - /Users/macbook/Documents/abc.py (3.8.2)
# Python program to find sum of elements in list
total = 0

# creating a list
list1 = [10, 20, 30, 40, 50]

# Taking a list and computing each element in Total
for ele in range(0, len(list1)):
    total = total + list1[ele]

# printing total value
print("Sum of all elements in given list: ", total)

print("program over")

|



                                                    Ln: 16   Col: 0
```

Output:

```
● ● ●                    Python 3.8.2 Shell
Python 3.8.2 (v3.8.2:7b3ab5921f, Feb 24 2020, 17:52:18)
[Clang 6.0 (clang-600.0.57)] on darwin
Type "help", "copyright", "credits" or "license()" for more information.
>>>
=================== RESTART: /Users/macbook/Documents/abc.py ===================
Sum of all elements in given list:  150
program over
>>> |


                                                    Ln: 8   Col: 4
```

Program #17

Program to print the summation of all numbers from 1 to N. Where N is the input.

```
# Program to add natural

# numbers upto n

# sum = 1+2+3+...+n where n is the input.

# To take input from the user

n = int(input("Please Enter n: "))

# initialize sum and counter

sum = 0

i = 1

while i <= n:

sum = sum + i

i = i+1 # update counter

# print the sum

print("The sum is", sum)
```

```
● ● ●        abc.py - /Users/macbook/Documents/abc.py (3.8.2)
# Program to add natural
# numbers upto n
# sum = 1+2+3+...+n where n is the input.

# To take input from the user
n = int(input("Please Enter n: "))

# initialize sum and counter
sum = 0
i = 1

while i <= n:
    sum = sum + i
    i = i+1     # update counter

# print the sum
print("The sum is", sum)

                                    Ln: 14   Col: 31
```

Output:

```
●  ●  ●                          Python 3.8.2 Shell
 Python 3.8.2 (v3.8.2:7b3ab5921f, Feb 24 2020, 17:52:18)
 [Clang 6.0 (clang-600.0.57)] on darwin
 Type "help", "copyright", "credits" or "license()" for more information.
 >>>
 ================== RESTART: /Users/macbook/Documents/abc.py ==================
 Please Enter n: 5
 The sum is 15
 >>> |
                                                              Ln: 8   Col: 4
```

Program #18

Program to input a number and check if it is a prime number.

```
# Program to check if an entered number is prime or not

num = int(input("Enter a number: "))

# prime numbers are numbers which have only two factors 1
and itself.

if num > 1:

# check for factors

for i in range(2,num):

if (num % i) == 0:

print(num,"is not a prime number")

break

else:

print(num,"is a prime number")

else:

print(num,"is not a prime number")
```

```
abc.py - /Users/macbook/Documents/abc.py (3.8.2)
# Program to check if an entered number is prime or not

num = int(input("Enter a number: "))

# prime numbers are numbers which have only two factors 1 and itself.
if num > 1:
    # check for factors
    for i in range(2,num):
        if (num % i) == 0:
            print(num,"is not a prime number")

            break
    else:
        print(num,"is a prime number")

else:
```
Ln: 15   Col: 28

```
Python 3.8.2 Shell
Python 3.8.2 (v3.8.2:7b3ab5921f, Feb 24 2020, 17:52:18)
[Clang 6.0 (clang-600.0.57)] on darwin
Type "help", "copyright", "credits" or "license()" for more information.
>>>
=================== RESTART: /Users/macbook/Documents/abc.py ===================
Enter a number: 121
121 is not a prime number
>>>
=================== RESTART: /Users/macbook/Documents/abc.py ===================
Enter a number: 7
7 is a prime number
>>>
```
Ln: 12   Col: 4

Program #19

Program to input a number and print its factors:

```python
# Python Program to find the factors of a given number
def print_factors(x):
    print("The factors of",x,"are:")
    for i in range(1, x + 1):
        if x % i == 0:
            print(i)
num = int(input("Please Enter n: "))
print_factors(num)
```

```
* abc.py - /Users/macbook/Documents/abc.py (3.8.2)*
# Python Program to find the factors of a given number

def print_factors(x):
    print("The factors of ",x,"are:")
    for i in range(1, x + 1):
        if x % i == 0:
            print(i)

num = int(input("Please Enter n: "))

print_factors(num)
```
Ln: 12   Col: 0

Output:

```
                      Python 3.8.2 Shell
Python 3.8.2 (v3.8.2:7b3ab5921f, Feb 24 2020, 17:52:18)
[Clang 6.0 (clang-600.0.57)] on darwin
Type "help", "copyright", "credits" or "license()" for more information.
>>>
=================== RESTART: /Users/macbook/Documents/abc.py ===================
Please Enter n: 10
The factors of 10 are:
1
2
5
10
>>>
=================== RESTART: /Users/macbook/Documents/abc.py ===================
Please Enter n: 20
The factors of 20 are:
1
2
4
5
10
20
>>>
```
Ln: 22   Col: 4

Program #20

Program to input a number and check if it is a Strong Number. A number is said to be Strong if it is equal to the sum of factorials of its digits.

Strong number is a special number whose sum of factorial of digits is equal to the original number. For example: 145 is strong number. Since, 1! + 4! + 5! = 145

Solution:

```
# Program to input a number and check if it is a strong number
sum1=0
num=int(input("Enter any number to check if it is a Strong Number:"))
tempnum=num
while(num):
i=1
f=1
r=num%10
while(i<=r):
f=f*i
i=i+1
sum1=sum1+f
num=num//10
if(sum1==tempnum):
print("The entered number is a strong number")
else:
print("The entered number is not a strong number")
```

```
abc.py - /Users/macbook/Documents/abc.py (3.8.2)
# Program to input a number and check if it is a strong number

sum1=0
num=int(input("Enter any number to check if it is a Strong Number:"))
tempnum=num
while(num):
    i=1
    f=1
    r=num%10
    while(i<=r):
        f=f*i
        i=i+1
    sum1=sum1+f
    num=num//10
if(sum1==tempnum):
    print("The entered number is a strong number")
else:
    print("The entered number is not a strong number")
                                                        Ln: 13    Col: 12
```

```
Python 3.8.2 Shell
Python 3.8.2 (v3.8.2:7b3ab5921f, Feb 24 2020, 17:52:18)
[Clang 6.0 (clang-600.0.57)] on darwin
Type "help", "copyright", "credits" or "license()" for more information.
>>>
================== RESTART: /Users/macbook/Documents/abc.py ==================
Enter a number:153
The number is not a strong number
>>>
================== RESTART: /Users/macbook/Documents/abc.py ==================
Enter a number:145
The number is a strong number
>>>
================== RESTART: /Users/macbook/Documents/abc.py ==================
Enter any number to check if it is a Strong Number:145
The entered number is a strong number
>>>
================== RESTART: /Users/macbook/Documents/abc.py ==================
Enter any number to check if it is a Strong Number:146
The entered number is not a strong number
>>> |
                                                        Ln: 20    Col: 4
```

AI with Python

Why Python is best for AI?

a. Less Code

b. Platform Independent

c. Massive Community Support

d. Ease of Learning

AI Applications are developed using various programming languages like Lisp, Prolog, C++, Java and Python. Among all, Python programming language is the most popular programming language for the AI applications.

Some of the reasons why Python is used for AI are as follows:

a. It has a simple syntax and requires less coding.

b. It has an inbuilt libraries for AI projects. For Example: Numpy, SciPy, matplotlib, nltk, SimpleAI are the major available inbuilt libraries of Python.

c. It is open source and can be used for a broad range of programming environments.

Use of Python in Pre-processing the Data

We need to follow the three steps to pre-process the data in Python:

a. Importing the useful packages using the import functions. We use the two packages NumPy and Sklearn.preprocessing.

b. Define the sample data using the preprocessing data.

c. Applying the preprocessing technique.

Python 3 and Scikit-learn which is a tool of machine learning are used for building a classifier in Python.

Logic Programming using Python

Python also provides a solution to solving the problems with Logic Programming. Logic Programming is one of the active principles of Artificial Intelligence. Here the language uses the two core components of Facts and Rules. The two packages Kanren and SymPy are used for logic programming in Python.

Applications of Logic Programming:

a. Solving Puzzles

b. Checking for Prime Numbers

c. Matching Mathematical Expressions

AI Assignments using Python Programming Language:

a. Gender Finder – Using the Python code to build a gender finder. We need to use a heuristic to construct a feature vector and train the classifer.

b. Category Prediction – Using the Python code to build a module which may predict whether a given sentence belongs to the category email, news or sports.

c. Analysis of Stock Market data. This is done using the necessary packages like matpotlib.finance which is inbuilt in Python.

d. Weather Forecast using Machine Learning.

Further Study: https://www.youtube.com/watch?v=7O60HOZRLng

Important Packages of Python used for AI:

These are the packages for deep learning, machine learning and data science. These libraries are perfect for using AI.

a. TensorFlow – This was developed by Google in collaboration with Brain Team. It is popularly used in writing Machine Learning algorithms. It is used for training multiple neural networks.

b. Scikit-Learn – It is a python library associated with NumPy and SciPy. It is considered as one of the best libraries for working with complex data. It is used for developing Unsupervised learning algorithms and Clustering. It also helps in feature extraction and image processing.

c. NumPy – It is considered as one of the most important machine learning libraries of Python. It is used for computing scientific/mathematical data. The most important feature of NumPy is its multi-dimensional array interface. It is widely used for statistical analysis. It is also used for expressing sound waves and images.

d. Theano – It is a python library that allows you to define, optimize and evaluate mathematical expressions involving multi-dimensional arrays efficiently. It allows a tight integration with NumPy. It is considered as a industry standard for research in Deep Learning and Neural Networks.

e. Keras – It is considered to be the most popular python package. It simplifies the implementation of neural networks. It also provides some of the best utilities for compiling models, processing data-sets, visualization of graphs and much more. It supports all the models of Neural Networks. It works well on both the CPU (Central Processing Unit) and the GPU (Graphics Processing Unit). It is completely Python based is easy to debug and explore.

f. NLTK – Natural Language Analyses Tool Kit, is an open source Python library for

Natural Language Processing, text analysis and text mining. It studies and analysis the Natural Language Text. It performs Text analysis and Sentimental Analysis.

AI Application Projects

Weather Forecast Using Machine Learning

Step 1:

Define the objective of the Problem – To predict the possibility of rain by studying the weather conditions.

What are we trying to predict?

What are the target featues?

What is the input data?

What kind of problem are we facing? Binary Classification/ Clustering?

Step 2:

Data Gathering – Data such as weather conditions, humidity level, temperature, pressure etc. are either collected manually or scarped from the web.

Step 3:

Data Preparation – This involves data cleaning and getting rid of inconsistencies like double values, missing values or redundant variables. It has a check for missing values, corrupted data and removal of unnecessary data.

Step 4:

Exploratory Data Analysis – This includes the understanding of the patterns and trends in the data. During this stage all the useful insights are drawn and correlations between the variables are made clear.

Step 5:

Building a Machine Learning Model – During this stage a predictive model is developed using the Machine Learning Algorithms such as Linear Regression, Decision Trees, etc.

Step 6:

Model Evaluation & Optimization – During this process the efficiency of the model is evaluated and any further improvement in the model are implemented. The accuracy of the model is calculated and further improvement in the model is done using the technique of Parameter tuning.

Step 7:

Predictions – The final outcome is predicted after performing the parameter tuning and improving the accuracy of the model in particular.

EXERCISE

Q1. Who developed Python?

Q2. What does Guido Van Rossum say about Python?

Q3. Write about various features of Python.

Q4. Name any two applications of Python.

Q5. Explain the term IDLE. Make use of www.python.org/ownloads/to download the IDLE.

Q6. Name the two modes of working in Python IDLE.

Q7. Explain the following with examples:

  a. Variables

  b. Data Types

  c. Operators

  d. Statements

  e. Functions

Q8. Name the data types of Number.

Q9. What are strings in Python.

Q10. Give the use of Lists in Python.

Q11. What is the use of Tuples in Python.

Q12. Explain the use of Sets in Python.

Q13. Give the use of Union in Sets in Python with an example.

Q14. Give the use of Intersection in Sets Python with an example.

Q15. Give the use of Difference in Sets Python with an example.

Q16. Write about the use of Dictionary in Python with an example.

Q17. Write about the various operators in Python.

Q18. Give any two examples of the following:

    a. Comparison Operators

    b. Assignment Operators

    c. Arithmetic Operators

    d. Identity Operators

    e. Membership Operators

    f. Conditional Statements

Q19. What is looping in Python. Name the various looping Statements of Python.

Q20. How does while loop differ from for. Explain with example programs.

Q21. What is a Nested Loop. Explain with the help of an example program.

Q22. Differentiate between BREAK and CONTINUE using example programs in Python.

Q23. What are functions in Python. How are they defined?

Q24. Write about the following:

    a. Defining a function.

    b. Creating a function.

    c. Calling a function.

Q25. Explain the use of input() function in Python using an example program.

Q26. Write a program in python to do the following:

    a. Input a number and check if it is an even number.

    b. Input a number and check if it is an even number.

    c. Input a number and check if it is a prime number.

Q27. Write a program in python to input a number and print its factors.

Q28. Write a program to print the table of all numbers from 1 to 10 till 10 terms.

Q29. Write a program to accept a number and print its reverse.

Q30. Write a program to store any ten numbers in an array and print the maximum and the minimum.

Q31. Write a program to print the sum of the following series:

    a. 1 + 2 + 3 + 4 + ...N where N is the input.

    b. 1 + 3 + 5 + 7 + N terms. Where N is the input.

Q32. Write a program to input a number and print its reverse.

Q33. Write a program to input a number and print the sum of its digits.

Q34. Write a program to input a number and print its factorial.

Q35. Write a program to input a name and print its reverse.

References

https://www.pexels.com/search/housing/

https://notionpress.com/read/basics-of-artificial-intelligence-machine-learning

www.Venturebeat.com

https://www.imaginovation.net/blog/artificial-intelligence-in-renewable-energy/

https://medium.com/computationallythinking/17-days-of-ai-for-good-sdg-8-decent-work-and-economic-growth-a9c1aced4008

https://hellofuture.orange.com/en/how-ai-can-help-reduce-inequalities/

https://arxiv.org/pdf/1905.00501.pdf

https://blogs.ei.columbia.edu/2018/06/05/artificial-intelligence-climate-environment/

https://www.recode.net/ad/18027288/ai-sustainability-environment

https://news.itu.int/3-ways-we-can-maximize-ais-impact-on-meeting-the-un-sustainable-development-goals/

http://cbseacademic.nic.in/web_material/Curriculum20/AI_Curriculum_Handbook.pdf

https://www.forbes.com/sites/bernardmarr/2018/09/28/artificial-intelligence-what-is-reinforcement-learning-a-simple-explanation-practical-examples/#6db38b07139c

https://www.youtube.com/watch?v=7O60HOZRLng

Books by the Same Author

Available at <u>amazon.com</u>

www.ingramcontent.com/pod-product-compliance
Lightning Source LLC
Chambersburg PA
CBHW051052050326
40690CB00006B/688

* 9 7 8 1 6 4 8 6 9 9 5 9 7 *